BINOCULARS

BINOCULARS

Masquerading as a Sighted Person

Philip F. DiMeo

NEW HORIZON PRESS
Far Hills, New Jersey

Requests for permission should be addressed to:
New Horizon Press
P. O. Box 669
Far Hills, NJ 07931

Philip F. DiMeo
    Binoculars: Masquerading as a Sighted Person

Cover design: Charley Nasta
Interior design: Scribe Inc.

Library of Congress Control Number: 2014950536

ISBN-13 (paperback): 978-0-88282-493-2
ISBN-13 (eBook): 978-0-88282-494-9

New Horizon Press

Manufactured in the U.S.A.

19   18   17   16   15   1   2   3   4   5

Author's Note

This book is based on the author's research, personal experiences, interviews and real life experiences. In order to protect privacy, names have been changed and identifying characteristics have been altered except for contributing experts.

For purposes of simplifying usage, the pronouns his/her and s/he are sometimes used interchangeably. The information contained in this book is not meant to be a substitute for professional evaluation and therapy with mental health professionals.

Table of Contents

Foreword

As a kid, I devoured books and stories about heroic animals. I never doubted the life-saving potential of our sweet family dog; Ginger's imaginary feats were extraordinary, her devotion unparalleled. But like most childhood notions, wondrous dreams of a transcendent human-animal bond faded and disappeared as I grew into adulthood. Then one damp and dreary afternoon during my senior year of college, I was reminded of those ideals and realized they were not just fantasy; I had my first encounter with a guide dog team on the "Miracle Mile" in downtown Chicago.

My recollection of that day is vivid. I had hurried out to grab lunch between classes, brooding about final exams and aiming for a cheap sandwich shop across Michigan Avenue. I fidgeted at the red light as horns blared and cars splashed past. Unexpectedly, the delicate and melodious jingle of dog tags cut through the soggy urban hum. A hefty, butter-colored Labrador retriever trotted toward the corner sporting a tan leather harness. A long handle rose from the strap across the dog's sturdy shoulders, and a man held the well-worn grip. The two weaved through pedestrians to stop at the curb alongside me, and the man reached down to scratch behind the dangling ears.

Forgetting my haste, I was both enthralled and alarmed. How will this dog know when it's safe to cross? Can he read the light? Should I help? Just as I made up my mind to speak, the light changed to green and the man confidently commanded the dog forward. My help was not needed. They crossed briskly to the other side and disappeared into a sea of umbrellas, leaving me in a state of awe.

The next time I saw a guide dog was four years later at the start of my career with Guide Dogs for the Blind, Inc. I learned what I didn't know that day in 1990: the guide dog did not decide when to cross the street. Instead, the man made the decision based on audible traffic flow, and the dog may have intelligently disobeyed his command if it wasn't safe to proceed. The flawless street crossing I had witnessed was a glimpse of the beautiful and complicated partnership that begins with a carefully bred, raised and trained guide dog, and a person who has established confidence and efficiency in independent travel.

At Guide Dogs for the Blind, an organization founded in 1942 primarily for servicemen blinded in combat in World War II, formal schooling to develop a guide dog's skills begins when the dogs are around a year-and-a-half old. But they are molded into well-mannered members of society from the start. As puppies, these guide dogs are carefully mentored and socialized from a young age while in the kennels on campus. At around eight weeks, each of the pups goes to the home of a volunteer puppy-raising family that teaches appropriate house behavior and shapes them into responsible young adults. Guide dog puppies accompany their raisers everywhere—from the boardroom to the classroom to the shopping mall—learning how to be calm and courteous in public settings. The dogs are then ready to return to the Guide Dogs campus for formal training.

The formal stage of training, using positive reinforcement methods, begins in a simple way. Using treadmill training with praise, a clicker and food reward, dogs are taught how to "lead" while wearing the Guide Dog harness. Complexity of training progresses in stages. Dogs develop the ability to lead their instructors in a straight line from point A to B along a sidewalk while maneuvering around obstacles along the way, to stop for curbs and changes in elevation such as steps or potential hazards, and to respond to directional commands ("Left" and "Right"). Throughout their education, the guide dogs learn to safely navigate a variety of environments from quiet, unpaved country roads to city subway platforms to college campuses to bustling urban centers. Proficiencies are tested with the Guide Dog Mobility Instructor under blindfold at several stages, before they are deemed ready to be paired with a student who comes to campus for a two-week course of instruction. The student is then shown the skills necessary to travel safely and efficiently with a guide dog, methods that they bring home after graduation to begin the process of growing into a smoothly working team. Prerequisites for this program include established mobility skills; a guide dog handler must already possess the confidence and independence to direct and manage the dog along a route, including making street-crossing decisions.

Gaining this type of independence can take tremendous courage and perseverance. Over the past two decades as a Guide Dog Mobility Instructor, I've met and worked with people who have overcome incredible odds and unfathomable challenges to regain or retain their independence without vision. The author of this book, Phil DiMeo, is one of them.

I met Phil in 2004 when he returned home from training, newly graduated with his first guide dog, Ladonna. Most guide dog teams encounter some hurdles along the way, especially during the first year; Phil and Ladonna were no exception. I watched them evolve as a team from their early days of establishing a bond and learning how to communicate with one another, to the later years of Ladonna's integral role in Phil's travels, social life and softball championships.

I am amazed by Phil's accomplishments, his abiding humor and unflappable courage. A compelling, vibrant individual, Phil's story offers encouragement through strength of will and a gritty approach to life's predicaments.

I have worked with hundreds of guide dog teams. Each pair has taught me valuable lessons about determination and self-awareness, partnership and empathy. Phil's engaging account of his own journey allows readers a chance to share in these insights and learn from his mistakes. His inspiring story illuminates his gradual migration from a devastating loss and a seemingly debilitating diagnosis to the effortless navigation of a smooth and skillful crossing on the Miracle Mile.

—Lauren Ross
Field Service Manager/Guide Dog Mobility Instructor
Guide Dogs for the Blind, Inc.
http://www.guidedogs.com

Chapter 1

Just Call Me Deadeye

At an early age I knew that something was wrong, something that made me different from the other kids. Little did I realize during my period of innocence that while my buddies were seeing objects in Technicolor on a wide screen in 3D and high definition, I was looking through a pair of binoculars, not seeing a lot of what was going on around me, unaware that my entire world was closing in on me.

It was at the age of four that I first became painfully aware of some of my visual problems. After playing in the yard of our home, I somehow unlatched the gate of our brown picket fence and darted out into the narrow lane next to my family's house, unaware that a car was coming toward me. Instinctively, I closed my eyes and dropped to the pavement at the sound of the blaring horn. When I opened my eyes, I found myself imprisoned under a massive steel body surrounded by four mammoth black tires. Just seconds later, I heard a loud scream from our upstairs tenant followed by the voice of the driver of the vehicle.

"Here, son," he said, as he reached down and extended his right arm. He grabbed my shoulder, gently slid me from under the car and lifted me up. The skin on my right elbow was bruised and smeared with blood. My father darted out of the house and thanked the man for his assistance.

I could sense my father's anger. I whimpered, telling him that the elbow stung. He said nothing. Roughly, he grabbed my left arm, yanked me onto the sidewalk, pulled me around the open gate and up the wooden steps into the kitchen where my mother was slumped over the stove crying. The pain from the skinned elbow was nothing compared to what I felt after my father whacked me across the neck and back.

My older sister Tana, my mother Grace, my father Philip and I lived in the rear of an old building, a grocery store which my father had converted into his music shop. An accomplished accordion player, he also taught others how to play. Since I was a junior, named after my father, Philip, I was given the nickname Butch.

My sister Tana and I often took the streetcar into downtown Milwaukee, where we walked up and down Wisconsin Avenue, had lunch at a department store's lunch counter and rode the elevators at another store. It was on one of those streetcars that my visual deficiencies resulted in my being separated from Tana.

On our ride back home, I couldn't locate Tana gesturing for me to follow her to the door at the front of the streetcar. Whenever we left the house, Tana held my hand. If for any reason she didn't and was on either side of me, I couldn't locate her. While she got off at the stop across from our house, I remained onboard, frantically scanning the area and hoping to spot her. What seemed like hours later, the streetcar finished its loop through town and stopped again across the street from our house. My mother, visibly shaken by the incident, was waiting. She hopped on immediately and led me back home.

During one Fourth of July celebration at Mitchell Park, I wandered away from my sister who was with her Girl Scout troop near the park pavilion. How I got lost I don't know but now, looking back, I'm sure it had to do with my vision. For over two hours I sat crying on the grass next to the lagoon, hoping someone would take me back to my sister. I heard my name blasted across the loudspeaker but didn't know where it was coming from. Finally, I was rescued by a middle-aged lady who grabbed my hand and led me back to my sister in the pavilion.

On Sundays, Tana and I went to The Pearl Theater, a small, dilapidated building packed with everyone from the neighborhood who enjoyed the Sunday matinees of Roy Rogers, Tarzan, The Bowery Boys and The Three Stooges. This amounted to four hours of entertainment for the price of one mere dime. We protested a few years later when the Pearl raised its admission price to a whopping twelve cents.

When I was six years old, I went to the Pearl with my sister and our neighbors on New Year's Eve. I nearly died that night. At first, it started with mild pains in my abdomen, then shot down to the groin area. By the time we reached the Pearl, the pain became so intense that I passed out and slept during much of the matinee. On the way home, I collapsed in the alley across from my house and was carried home by one of the neighbors. I awoke on my living room couch listening to my mother calling my father, who was performing at a party in Waukesha, about twenty miles from where we lived. During a furious snowstorm, my father raced home, wrapped me in a blanket and drove me to the hospital, where I underwent emergency appendectomy surgery.

"Had you not taken your son to the hospital, he would have been dead in four hours," said the doctor who performed the surgery.

Those matinees at the Pearl were my escape from the problems at home that usually erupted on Sundays. While we were at the Pearl, my father went to the east side of Milwaukee to visit his mother and sisters. Mother stayed home and drank father's wine, brandy or whatever was in our pantry.

I loved cowboy movies. My favorite cowboys were Roy Rogers, Gene Autry, Rocky Lane and Rex Allen. My childhood fantasy was—and still is—to go out west and ride horses on a ranch. During the cold winters, I fantasized about being a cowboy and pretended the alleys I walked through were western towns—the frozen snowbanks were the boulders and hills featured in those black and white B-westerns.

My love of comic books began at the age of eight; that's when I was introduced to the Sunday funnies. Flash Gordon and The Phantom were my favorites.

Soon, I discovered the ultimate comic book store one mile from my house. For five cents, one could purchase two comics with covers or six without covers. Each day, I put change into a small leather pouch and on Saturday mornings I'd buy as many comics as I could. Then I'd stuff them into the yellow saddlebag of my three-speed racer and peddle home with my stash.

I became hooked on superheroes. There was Superman, Plastic Man, The Flash, The Green Lantern, Aquaman, Wonder Woman and my all-time favorite, Batman.

Not only did I spend hours reading and re-reading the comics, but I was constantly drawing the characters. Later, I created my own superheroes; Mastermind, the robot from outer space ,and Solarman, whose superpowers emanated from a solar disk on his chest. (He was the first green energy superhero!)

I continued to have vision problems. I was told a weak or crossed left eye was at the root of all my problems. I often got in scuffles with those who called me cross-eyed. So enraged was I after the neighborhood bully referred to me as a cross-eyed freak that I hit him over the head with one of my sister's batons. At the age of five, I was fitted by a specialist with my first pair of corrective glasses: a crude pair of wire-rims, often broken during scuffles with other boys. In second grade I graduated to tan plastic-rimmed glasses but the results remained the same. It seemed as if I was always going to get new glasses.

I loved playing softball. Because inner-city playgrounds lacked space, a large ball (fourteen inches) had to be used to restrict its flight. Despite the large balls and the high fence, many balls ended up on the sidewalk, street and even on someone's porch. Little kids cheered watching the older boys, some of whom were in their mid-twenties, launching those large rubber-coated balls, which sometimes broke windows. The front window of a small grocery store across from

Alexander Mitchell playground was a favorite target. The older boys often took bets on who would be the first to shatter the front window. When not on a playground, we played twelve-inch softball in a small gravel area next to an alley. White birch trees surrounded the area, once a playground. A large elm separated right and left field. The rusty metal frame of an old swing set served as the outfield fence. Over the swing set was an automatic home run but if you hit the ball into one of the yards, you were out. I was great in a confined area like the gravel lot, but on a playground or a ball field, I had problems. I didn't understand that, unlike the other boys, I was operating in a very narrow universe the size of a phone booth—anything out of that universe like a ball, a tree or even a person was lost.

Most of the balls hit in the yards either broke garage or house windows or were confiscated by angry homeowners. Many of the games ended when the police were called and a squad car entered the alley.

"Beat it, the cops are here!" was our cue to scatter.

When I was eight years old, my father took me to my first major league baseball game. We sat in the lower grandstands at the newly built Milwaukee County Stadium to cheer on our new team—the Braves that had moved to Milwaukee from Boston.

I sipped his beer and chomped on hot dogs that somehow were tastier than the ones cooked at home. With my mitt on my lap, I anticipated catching a foul ball like many of my friends but never did. I loved watching infield practice and marveled at how third baseman Eddie Mathews smoothly scooped up the ball from what looked like a green carpet and rifled it over to Billy Joe Adcock at first. I saw Hall of Fame pitcher Warren Spahn on the mound tossing looping curveballs to Del Crandall behind the plate. From where I sat, the ball appeared to be in slow motion.

Locating ground balls cracking off the bats was difficult. I rarely saw popups or fly balls and never glimpsed home runs.

"Did you see that?" my father often asked after a long home run from Eddie Mathews or Billy Joe Adcock.

"No," I shamefully replied.

"Concentrate," was my father's standard response.

We attended several times (all afternoon games) and it was always the same. I seldom saw fly balls, never saw home runs and never snagged a foul ball. My vision was significantly worse than anyone knew.

Chapter 2

See No Evil

I attended St. Adalbert's Catholic grade school for six years. At first, church frightened me. It wasn't merely the holy objects like the statues or the candles and the priest at the altar but the darkness; I had trouble navigating in the dimly lit church.

St. Adalbert's, an old Catholic school, served the predominantly Polish residents of the area. At St. Adalbert's, we were required to attend mass before our regular classes. We reported to school at 7:30 A.M. and stood in rows of two waiting for a nun to march us, like toy soldiers, to the huge yellow church where we spent an hour listening to Father Gusheski or Father Zeke, whose services were in his native Polish. Walking behind Sister in a group was okay with me. As long as I was following someone, I could not get lost. That was my greatest fear—losing someone to the side of me and getting lost.

During the morning mass, I played with my fingers, daydreamed or used my holy rosary to lasso the purses of unsuspecting girls.

It was in Sister Irmina's kindergarten class that I first learned my real name.

"Aren't you Philip DiMeo?" she asked.

"No, that's my dad—my name is Butch."

I also learned my first prayer—The Hail Mary.

With a bent piece of cardboard draped over my head for a helmet and a tree branch for a rifle, I acted as one of six wooden soldiers in my first school play. Sister Irmina played an old recording of *The March of the Wooden Soldiers* while we stomped onto the stage and around a large wooden stump. The shadowy stage frightened me—I wasn't afraid of the dark but that I would trip. For my second and last performance, I was one of four minstrels in another musical.

My First Holy Communion, the big event of my life at that time, took place on a hot Sunday morning in late May. After the mass, my parents met me in the lobby and we all proudly walked to our house where Tana took pictures. There I was, pure of heart and all decked out in my blue communion suit, a white shirt and a pair of brand new brown shoes with yellow crepe soles.

As a youth I strived to be the best at everything. I was the best tree climber, fastest runner, best arm wrestler and could usually whip most in my age bracket. Sports, however, were a different story. I had the strongest arm when it came to throwing things like baseballs, footballs and snowballs—I broke many a streetlight with my strong, accurate throws. When it came to catching things, however, I had problems. My interest in competitive sports began in the fifth grade. Since St. Adalbert's had no playground, we often took a rubber ball and threw it against the old brick building in the gravel area. I had trouble catching the ball as it bounced off the bricks. Others always cut in front of me and caught the ball while I waited for it. It was bad enough that most of the boys were better than me, but one girl always beat me to the ball too. Was my weak left eye responsible or something else?

I tried my hand at basketball at the social center. No matter what I did, the ball was always swiped or taken away from me. I also had difficulty fielding bounce passes from my teammates; I kept asking myself, what was the problem?

Since the sisters at St. Adalbert's prohibited athletic equipment on the school grounds, I used one of the batons from the display case in my father's music store as a bat. At noon recess, I'd hit the rubber ball against the building and then try to catch it. My one-man baseball activities were terminated one afternoon when Sister Rose seized the baton.

In fifth grade, Sister Rose asked me if I would be interested in being a ballplayer in a play she was directing. My difficulty locating the ball the boys on stage were tossing around at the first rehearsal convinced me that a play which required me to catch a ball or anything else was not for me, unfortunately.

During a game of tackle at noon recess, I tore the cartilage in my left knee. I was hospitalized for one week and the doctors wanted to perform knee surgery. I refused the surgery after hearing from the doctor himself that I would walk with a permanent limp. When I returned to St. Adalbert's on crutches, Sister Rose assigned the tallest, stockiest boy in the class to assist me. Mike helped me up and down stairs, walked me home and even followed me into the bathroom, making sure I didn't fall into the toilet while doing my business.

After six years at St. Adalbert's, I asked to go to a different school. I wanted to attend Alexander Mitchell public school, the school where many of my friends went to classes.

"You can go to public school after your confirmation," my mother promised.

Chapter 3

That Wonderful Year

Growing up, I had many boyhood heroes. At first, they were the cowboys featured in those Sunday matinees and on television and then later, baseball players. However, my greatest hero of all wasn't Roy Rogers, Gene Autry, The Cisco Kid (whom I had met), Hank Aaron or even Bart Starr, but my sixth-grade teacher, Mr. Mueller.

On a cool September morning, I stepped onto the Alexander Mitchell School playground, ready to begin a new chapter in my life; I would be a real public school student. I would be with many of my friends every day.

Despite my attire—a tan checkered sport coat, a white shirt and a bowtie—I managed to participate in a touch football game. I drew the praise of

Jerry Gronowski after catching one of his passes for the winning touchdown.

"Did you see goo-goo eyes catch my bullet pass?" he boasted. Actually, the pass wasn't a bullet pass and I never really saw it—all I know is that when I turned around, the ball somehow ended up on my right hip. That catch made me an instant celebrity at school. So elated was I that I didn't even mind Jerry referring to me as "goo-goo eyes."

Richie, my neighborhood buddy, told me about sixth-grade teacher Mr. Mueller; about his having the entire solar system hanging from his ceiling and how he often took his class out onto the playground to play softball and football. During summer registration, I requested that Mr. Mueller be my sixth-grade teacher and two weeks later I received my answer: On the first day of school, I was to report to Robert Mueller in Room 105.

After the touch football game, I sprinted to the building in anticipation of my first meeting with Mr. Mueller. My enthusiasm was tempered within moments of entering the dark building, since I belly-flopped down a flight of old wooden steps.

I wasn't about to let that setback stop me. I brushed the dust from my sportcoat, straightened my bow tie and headed for my classroom, stopping at every doorway to read the room numbers: 100, 101, 102, 103, 104 and 105—R. Mueller.

Upon entering the room, I looked up and there it was: the entire solar system hanging from the ceiling, just as Richie had described. The papier-mâché celestial figures were proportional to the dimensions of the real planets themselves. At the center was a large orange sun followed by a yellow planet Mercury, a light blue Venus, a green and blue Earth, a red Mars, a huge blue Jupiter, a gray Saturn with three cardboard rings, a dark blue Uranus, a green Neptune and a white Pluto.

"Hey, Phil!" a familiar, low-pitched voice called from the back of the room.

There was no mistaking that voice—it was either a talking frog or Jules, a neighborhood friend whom I had met through Richie. Jules was at the last desk playing with a magnet and metal soldiers. I sat down alongside him.

While Jules played with the magnet, my eyes were fixated on the front of the room, waiting for Mr. Mueller. I recognized some of the boys, most of whom I knew through Richie. Then in walked Mr. Mueller himself. He looked just as I had pictured him, just as Richie described him. He was dressed conservatively, wearing a brown suit, a thin brown tie and a white shirt. He wore tan rimmed glasses and his brown hair was cut short.

He introduced himself, then gave a short lecture on his expectations for the class. He talked about citizenship, morality and self-pride. He told us that along with the regular subjects like math and English, we would learn about sports, particularly football, softball and basketball. He was everything I thought a man should be.

He strolled toward my desk and confronted Jules, still fixated on those goofy metal soldiers.

"Wasn't it bad enough that you flunked my class last semester? Do you want to flunk again?" he asked sternly.

"And you," he said, turning to me. "Why would you hang around with a boy who flunked sixth grade?"

Swell, I thought, *I'm in his class for only a few minutes and already Mr. Mueller's criticizing me.*

He told us of his policy that allowed students who completed an assignment during class time to read any book from his library located along the rear wall of the room. The first book I read was about Joe, who bet his friends that he could survive for three months in the wilderness without any provisions or clothes. In June, Joe was dropped off in a secluded area in Canada and was to be picked up sometime in September. Joe made tools out of stone, built a shelter out of mud, leaves and branches and made crude spears, bows and arrows to kill rabbits and deer for food and clothing. When his friend returned in November, he found Joe thin, with shoulder-length hair and a long beard but in good physical condition. I fantasized about surviving in the wilderness.

"Someday, I'm going to do that," I told one of my classmates.

Every day after I finished my classwork, I headed for the bookshelves, seeking science books about dinosaurs and astronomy, specifically the planets. I learned everything I could about the solar system, the distances of planets from the sun, the composition of their atmospheres and the number of moons circling each planet. I was fascinated with the planet Mars, which at that time was believed to have some type of life.

For my first book report, which was oral, I chose *Inside The Space Ships*, by George Adamski, who told about his encounters with alien beings. In *Inside The Space Ships*, Adamski recounted his first meeting in a California bar with two men, one from the planet Venus and the other from Mars. With his permission, the men drove him to what he described as a large blue metallic object, hidden in a remote area of the California desert. He went on to say the men invited him onboard, allowing him to examine the spacecraft. In the book were black and white photos of a glowing cigar-shaped Venusian mother ship and a saucer-shaped Venusian scout ship.

"Do you believe the book?" a classmate, Gloria, asked.

"I think the author is full of it." I took one look at Mr. Mueller, seated in the rear, shaking his head. "I mean, I don't believe him."

During the second week of school, Mr. Mueller surprised the class when he stood up from his desk and told us that we needed a break from our schoolwork. "Since you have conducted yourselves in an orderly manner, we're all going to go on to the playground and play football."

After chastising and kicking off the playground four teenage boys who were smoking and drinking beer, he divided the class into two lines, one for passing the football and one for catching it. We used a rubber playground football, smaller and easier for our hands to grip. He taught us to place our fingers on the large seam of the ball with the index finger on the back. He then brought the ball to his ear and threw—all perfect spirals. I'll always remember standing behind him, with his dark tie waving in the breeze while he effortlessly threw those perfect passes.

I always had a very strong arm and, with the exception of Mr. Mueller, was able to throw the football harder and farther than anyone in the sixth grade. However, I was unable to throw the football with my index finger in the back the way Mr. Mueller taught us to.

Catching that playground ball was another matter. I dropped several of Mr. Mueller's passes. He eased my frustration by having me toss the ball to the other boys. *Why couldn't I catch like the other boys? Why was I different from the other boys?*

In November, Mr. Mueller held a passing contest measuring distance and accuracy.

Despite not throwing the ball the way Mr. Mueller had taught us, I easily won the contest. Two weeks later, Mr. Mueller presented me with an award: a blue ribbon and a framed certificate with the inscription *Philip DiMeo, Passing Champion of Alexander Mitchell School, 1956.*

He also took us to the playground basketball court and taught us how to shoot layups. We'd stand in a line, wait for his bounce pass, then dribble to the basket to hopefully bank the ball off the backboard and into the hoop.

During the winter months, Mr. Mueller took the entire class up into an attic room that served as his gymnasium. Standing to the right side of a large mat, he directed us to run and tumble forward, then return to the back of the line. The tumbling was so much fun that no one objected to how cold and dusty it was in that attic. It was also dark. When tumbling, I always stood in the back of the line waiting for my eyes to clear.

On warm spring days, we played softball on the playground. Mr. Mueller and one of his student teachers were the team captains.

Mr. Mueller started each day with current events. We were each to report on an article we had read in the *Milwaukee Journal* or *Milwaukee Sentinel.* I once got in trouble for trying to fake a report on an article about an artesian well.

Mr. Mueller showed slides and we were supposed to identify political figures. Many of us were able to identify President Eisenhower and Vice President Nixon but only one student was able to identify Egypt's Abdul Nasser.

We also viewed slides of other continents, like Africa and India.

"Those people are starving," Mr. Mueller said. "By the year 2000, there will be over two billion people in the world and not enough food to feed them."

It was at Mitchell school that I developed my friendship with Dave—everyone called him "Slim." I had seen him around the neighborhood but it wasn't until my second week at Mitchell that we became good friends. We walked to school, ate lunch and walked home together. He even persuaded me to join him on the audio-visual crew.

"It's easy," he said, demonstrating how to thread a movie projector.

Not only was I unable to see the film, I couldn't see Slim, the projector or anything else in the dark room. I frequently bumped into chairs and once nearly knocked the projector off the table. That incident convinced me that the audio-visual crew was not for me.

In October, we had a Halloween costume party. Most of my classmates came as hobos. I wore the Superman outfit Tana had bought me while I was recuperating from my knee injury the previous year. I couldn't help smiling at several of the girls wearing old coats and hats with their faces smeared with coal.

We marched around the building, surrounded by cheering neighbors and parents.

"Hey, mommy, there's Superman!" shouted a young boy, pointing at me.

On Tuesdays and Thursdays, we had music class with Mrs. Evans, a gray-haired lady whose room was across the hall. Mrs. Evans played the piano and sang. She taught us songs in preparation for the Christmas program in December.

The boys were divided into two groups, alto and soprano. Like my sister Tana, an accomplished opera singer, I was soprano. During that period in my life, I possessed a very good singing voice—I had no doubt that I would be selected for the Christmas program. However, I was crushed when I was one of only three boys not chosen.

In March, we started rehearsal for the all-city music festival that was to take place in May. At first, we rehearsed in Mrs. Evan's room; later, we walked to another school to rehearse with Mr. Heiden, the all-city director. We learned such songs as *I'm Always Chasing Rainbows, I Love A Parade, There Are Smiles* and even *Holy, Holy, Holy* (In those days, there wasn't a problem with religion in public schools). My favorite of all the songs was *They Call It America, But I Call It Home.*

I practiced hard to impress Mrs. Evans—she assured me that I would be singing in the festival.

On a warm May morning, we boarded the school bus for the arena in downtown Milwaukee. Mrs. Evans and Mr. Mueller sat up front near the driver; I sat in the rear next to my friends Sharon and Slim. We were dropped off in front of the Milwaukee Arena. Mrs. Evans seemed nervous as she led us into the building and to our seats.

"Don't worry Mrs. Evans, they'll do fine," assured Mr. Mueller.

Cautiously I followed behind Sharon, fearful that I would bump into something or trip one of the girls.

We took our places and sat silently. Mr. Heiden raised his baton and we started singing. The first song was *Holy, Holy, Holy*, followed by a song about the American Eagle. I glanced over at Sharon, standing to my left—she looked as if she was in agony. Her face was shiny; sweat was streaming down her forehead. The more we sang, the calmer I became. We ended the program with *They Call It America* and then stood proudly, listening to the shouts, whistles and a thunderous ovation from the eight thousand plus in the audience. Several of the girls broke out into tears—two embraced each other crying. It took every ounce of self-control to hold back my tears. It was an unbelievable experience. I didn't want it to end. Mrs. Evans came over to us and told us how proud she was. Mr. Mueller was beaming. It was one of the happiest moments of my life.

On the last day of class, we gave out gifts and signed each other's photo albums, a small notebook with individual black-and-white pictures and a class photo with Mr. Mueller's head in the upper right-hand corner. After the 11 A.M. dismissal, I went up to Mr. Mueller and thanked him for everything he had done for me.

"I'll never forget you," I said tearfully.

He smiled and grabbed my hand. "Philip, I want you to come back and see old Mr. Mueller again."

"I will, I promise."

Unfortunately for me, I waited too long. When I returned to the Alexander Mitchell School twenty years later, a plaque had been placed on the door of Mr. Mueller's old room in his honor after his passing: ROBERT MUELLER, BELOVED TEACHER AT ALEXANDER MITCHELL SCHOOL. That plaque brought back all those wonderful memories. Teary eyed, I stood staring at the plaque. "Sorry, Mr. Mueller," I whispered. "I should have come back sooner."

Chapter 4

School Days

Playing it cool at a school with high standards like Walker, where I went to school next, was no easy task, especially with my growing vision problems. Because of the wide hallways and large groups of students shuffling back and forth coupled with my narrow visual field, I became disoriented and had trouble finding my homeroom. My teacher watched me arrive late and said I would have to pay more attention to the rules. I became so embarrassed that I ran out of the room and slid down three or four of those hard wide marble steps. After composing myself in the bathroom, I waited for the students to leave, then went back to the room to apologize to her. She was gracious and accepted the apology. Later, I was one of a few selected for an accelerated or high achievement class in which the expectations were a lot higher than the other classes. I never knew why I was placed in an accelerated class but I suspected Mr. Mueller had recommended me.

At noon, I strolled over to the park directly across from the school, where I ran into my neighborhood pal Roger who, along with two other boys, was playing catch with a small rubber ball. Upon seeing me, he whizzed the ball, which I never saw, past my nose.

Unlike Mitchell, where I felt comfortable and safe, in my first months at Walker I felt alone and kept to myself. I missed many of my grade school buddies.

In the second semester of seventh grade I took, as part of the manual arts requirements, a woodworking course taught by Mr. Shephard. For our first project, we were to take a large flat piece of wood and by planing both sides, it would become a breadboard. *Simple enough*, I thought. However, with my eye difficulties and the requirements of school courses growing, absolutely nothing was simple. Not only did tunnel vision prevent me from seeing the entire surface but lack of depth perception confused me; I couldn't tell which side was higher than the other. I'd plane one side thinking it was the entire board, go to the other side and then start all over again. While the other boys were working on their third and fourth projects like constructing drawers and cabinets, I was still trying to plane the board.

Mr. Shephard, through the goodness of his heart, not only finished planing it but gave me a B for the course. At that time, I was unaware that my eyes were the underlying problem. I thought the breadboard incident was due to my manual skill deficiencies.

My favorite class was art, taught by Mrs. Green. During the third week, I brought her Mastermind the Robot and Solarman, the two comic book superhero characters I had created the previous year. She was impressed and told me that I had a future in cartooning.

During this period my mother was hospitalized because of an emotional breakdown and I fell into a deep depression. My grade point average dropped from close to an A to a D. I was transferred from the accelerated class into the lowest achievement class. I often spent much of the night wandering the streets and alleys until 2:00 or 3:00 A.M. During that awful period, both my father and Tana were seldom home. Tana often spent the evening with the neighbors across the street and weekends with our aunt.

Rather than bike home after school one afternoon, I headed down 43rd Street. When I reached Highway 24, I turned right and sped southward into the open country, furiously peddling past cornfields, wooded areas and farmhouses. Pumping my legs as hard as I could, I roared down a steep hill. A feeling of exhilaration and freedom consumed me as I knifed through torrents of wind. At the bottom I spotted a large brown sign with yellow letters: *Root River Parkway*. That was my destination.

I peddled along what was then a gravel road, listening to the birds, crickets and the chorus from the frogs hidden among the large willows, lily pads and cattails that lined the nearby Root River. I crossed a narrow wooden bridge and stopped briefly at an old, dilapidated shack. Alongside the shack was one of those old metal water pumps. After leaning the bike against the shack, I firmly grasped the handle, thrust myself forward and pulled up and pressed down, up and down, up and down until my arms, back and shoulders tired. Then I dropped to my knees and waited. Like the flood gates of a dam opening or a fire hydrant after the nozzle has been removed, the water shot out of the rusty gray pipe. Making like a pioneer or one of my cowboy heroes, I slurped and gulped from the palms of my cupped hands and, with each gulp, savored the cold, metallic-flavored liquid.

Now it was getting dark and I needed a place to spend the night. First, I considered going home; however, it was a long ride back and I was too tired, so I dismissed that idea. I walked the racer along several trails and came upon a small pond at the base of a heavily wooded hillside—it was perfect. Fearing someone would spot me, I hid the racer in a thicket of shrubs and spent the cool clear autumn evening nestled in a clump of weeds beneath a large willow tree.

On weekends, we visited mother and took her to the restaurant across from the hospital. It was depressing—with each visit she'd ask when she was coming home. She remained at the hospital until the following March and then returned home.

Throughout this time, I kept up with my cartooning. A fellow musician friend of my father who had his own printing company promised to publish a comic about my character, Mazy. His promise inspired me to sacrifice my eighth grade homework in order to finish *Mazy*. I spent hours drawing at the kitchen table, using a fountain pen filled with black India ink.

After two arduous months of pen-and-ink drawings, forty-four pages and a 1.5 grade point average at Walker Junior High, I presented *Mazy* to my father's friend, who did not treat it seriously. It turned out that he'd just been joking and had never planned to publish my comic. I was heartbroken.

In gym class, I continued having vision problems that I didn't understand. I had difficulty locating the large volleyball when we played. I sometimes saw the ball coming straight at me but never could locate it if it was thrown from my right or left. I tried out for the softball team as a pitcher, but the coach put me in left field. My hitting was adequate but my lack of depth perception caused problems with my fielding. After I misjudged two fly balls, the coach promptly cut me from the team.

A bunch of us who didn't make the team started our own intramural team—naturally, I became the coach and made myself the pitcher. We scheduled a game against the school's team. At first the coach was reluctant to play a bunch of losers but, on the urging of his players, accepted the challenge.

The coach thought that there was no way we were going to win the game. The contest took place on a Friday after school on the asphalt diamond behind the building. We gave it a valiant effort but lost 10–7. I pitched a good game and my hitting was outstanding. I went four for four with two doubles, a single and a home run. However, it was my two slides into second base on the rough, hard asphalt that really impressed the coach.

After the game I shook hands with the coach, who praised my performance.

At the age of thirteen, my friend Richie and I formed a hardball team. We went around the neighborhood signing up players, most of whom were our own age. One boy, a real natural at every sport, signed up several of his buddies, all older than the rest of us. Not only did these guys join the team, they took it over. He immediately informed us that not only would he be the starting pitcher and leadoff batter, but also the manager as well. Impressed with my speed along with my throwing arm, our "manager" mistakenly started me in left field.

In theory it should have worked. I was fast and my arm was strong and accurate but there was one problem: I couldn't see the ball. That was apparent when, in the second inning of our first game, I failed to locate a routine fly ball. At first, I heard the sound of the ball coming off the bat, then heard our "manager's" screechy voice bitching at me; that's when I realized I was in trouble. I knew the ball was hit to me but couldn't locate it. I ran in, then backpedaled. Though I never saw the ball, I managed to catch a glimpse of three runners crossing home plate. I was pulled from the game, loudly chewed out and then cut. Totally humiliated, I left the field with my mitt tucked under my right arm and, teary eyed, walked the two miles back home alone, vowing never to play hardball again.

I tried out as a guard for the school basketball team instead. I considered myself a great shooter; I sunk thirty-nine baskets in a row to win a free-throw shooting contest at school. But on the court in a real game, it was a different story. I could not handle the ball. Whatever I did, I had the ball stolen while dribbling—I never saw the defender swiping at the ball and I couldn't figure it out. I dropped off the Walker team and joined an after-school intramural team. The results were the same: the ball was always swiped from me. I had no idea that it was my lack of peripheral vision causing the problem. In fact, at that time I didn't even know what peripheral vision was.

One day I was struck on the side of my right eye with a rubber ball. Moments later, I noticed what appeared to be a floating speck in that eye and told my father. He took me to a specialist; the doctor concluded after three days of extensive testing that the optic nerve was slightly bruised with no serious damage to the eye. He even went so far as to say my eyes would continue to grow and my vision would improve. He was right—at the age of nineteen, every aspect of my straight ahead vision improved; without glasses, my vision was a respectable 20/30. Despite the reassurances that my vision was improving, down deep, I knew something was wrong, something that separated me from others.

When I entered South Division High, I still had the light-to-dark problem, going from the bright outside into the dark building. But after a few weeks, I became familiar with the building entrances and was able to negotiate the stairways and corridors without difficulty.

I enrolled in a beginner's judo class. The class, taught by a first degree black belt, met on Tuesdays, Thursdays and Saturdays at the Milwaukee Eagles Club. Rather than learn throws or how to beat the hell out of somebody, we spent the first six weeks just learning how to fall.

During the sixth week, I noticed a man who was standing near the gym entrance staring at me. The way he looked and the way he was dressed—a dark pinstriped suit, a dark shirt and light colored tie—I concluded that he was a gangster. After the class, he approached me with what he called a proposition.

The short, stocky man with the broken nose introduced himself as Joe Fontain, a former middleweight boxer. His proposition: to train me to compete in the Golden Gloves.

"With my training, you could be a lightweight champion," he said.

Strangely, my father, an amateur boxing champion who had trained his nephew for the Golden Gloves, was not too keen on Fontain or his proposition. Since I was bored with the judo class, I decided to try my hand at boxing.

For the first two weeks I worked out with weights, jumped rope and practiced on the body and speed bags and sparred a little with Frankie, one of Fontain's ex-students. During the third week, he set up a match with another one of his students, a tall, thin boy. With no mouthpiece and no headgear in the small ring above the Eagles gym, we were to go three rounds with one minute intervals. For the first two rounds, we danced around lightly jabbing at each other.

"Whatsamatter?" shouted Fontain. "You guys going steady or something? Now get out there and hit each other. This is no dance social!"

The other boy came out swinging; he really laid it on me. Midway through the last round, he landed a left hook to the side of my head; that really set me off. I crouched down and pummeled his mid section with hard body punches, then landed a right uppercut.

"That's the way to go," shouted Fontain. "You were great, Phil!"

And I felt great too. That is until I looked down and saw my opponent sprawled out on the mat, unconscious.

"Oh, man. I killed him!" I shouted.

"Oh, he'll be alright," Fontain replied, trying to calm me.

Fontain had one of his trainers drive me home while they attended to my opponent. Two days later, my judo instructor informed me that my opponent was taken to St. Mary's Hospital where he was treated for a broken jaw. Though I continued with judo for another year, I vowed to never fight again.

My sister Tana's wedding was planned for October 16. The wedding party consisted of her fiancée's brother, cousin and me. I dreaded being part of the wedding—I feared screwing up or knocking something over in the dark church but the ceremony went off without my having a problem.

At South, there were two gym teachers. Unlike the well-built one who had transferred from Walker like me and stressed calisthenics, the other's method of molding young men's bodies, of getting them into peak physical condition, consisted of his pounding the floor with a window pole while the class duck-walked around the gym. Having sustained a serious knee injury, I pointed out to this coach that deep squats and duck walking could result in damage to the knee cartilage.

"You think you know more than me, DiMeo?" he barked back.

My refusal to answer that question or participate in duck-walking landed me in the principal's office.

The coaches at South were no better. At our first football practice, we were told by the coach that our helmet was a weapon; to lead with the helmet. No one seemed aware of the danger of concussions or neck or spinal injuries.

As bad as the coaching was, the equipment we were given was worse. The helmets, hand-me-downs from the varsity, were ill-fitting. Many of them, like the one they gave me, had no face bars. The pants had no knee or thigh pads. The shoes, old black high-tops with long spikes, were frayed and the toes curled upward.

At the first practice I thought I dazzled the coaches with my sixty-five-yard passes until I was inserted at left defensive tackle. Despite cutting most of the practices, I was given a set of letters at the sports banquet.

During my teen years, my eyesight seemed to me to be the best it had ever been. However, an incident occurred during my junior year that should have served as a warning of what was to follow in later life. During the spring, boys' gym classes were allowed to play softball on the football practice field alongside the building. Entering the dark school building after one such game, I tumbled down a flight of hard marble steps.

"What the hell happened to you, DiMeo?" barked my gym teacher from behind me.

"I didn't see the steps," I sheepishly replied.

Rather than help me up, he leaned over me and inquired as to why the hell I wanted to play sports if I couldn't see.

It was the old light-to-dark adaptation thing again. Going from the bright sunlight to the dim building had caused the problem. However, I dismissed the incident as another problem caused by a weak left eye.

It was in high school that I renewed my friendship with Brick, an old St. Adalbert's buddy. Also in high school, my interest in cartooning became an obsession. In my tenth grade art class, a Russian artist was to assist our art teacher. His specialty was watercolor paintings of boats and ships in marina settings. I created a watercolor masterpiece of sailboats in a harbor. The instructor was impressed with the painting until I added a Nazi submarine chasing a swimmer and a figure in a diving suit being attacked by sharks. The instructor became so infuriated that he demanded that I leave the class.

Brick, his mother, father and brother occupied the first floor of a small wooden cottage. Unlike my house, where my parents constantly yelled, Brick's parents seldom spoke to each other. I recall spending hours at his house where rarely a word was spoken.

Brick's father was a junk dealer in a nearby village. He could often be observed kneeling with a lit cigarette dangling out of the side of his mouth, dipping a rusty piece of metal into a pan of gasoline. Many of the residents in the old south side neighborhood wagered on when he would blow himself up. Brick often helped to keep his father supplied with metal, tires or whatever he could scrounge up.

*   *   *

In my junior year, my friend Slim and I took a speech class. Our teacher was one of three with hearing deficits. At the start of her class she turned up her hearing aids. During one of my speeches, I impersonated the vice principal addressing the school during a fire. As the building was burning, she was making announcements over the loud-speaker. "Everyone remain seated until I dismiss you. If you are not perfectly quiet, you will have to remain in your seats."

With the exception of the speech teacher, who probably couldn't hear what I was saying, my speech drew thunderous laughter.

After the speeches, the class would make comments such as "good diction" or "good flow." Slim and I made up our own comments: "that was good raptentious dipardulation" and "your demineum delecteon was negligible."

"All right," was our teacher's standard response.

When my name was called for the final speech of the term, I walked to the front of the class, pulled out a blank index card and placed it on the podium, took out a hankie to clean my glasses and looked up at the class and pretended I was speaking. I rotated my head from side to side, moved my mouth and made animated hand gestures, like I was really speaking. I looked toward the teacher, who, with a puzzled expression, kept straining her head toward me and fidgeting with her hearing aid. Everyone in the class laughed. The more they laughed, the more animated I became. I pounded the podium and raised my right hand in the air. After about twenty minutes I picked up my index card and placed it in my pocket.

Everyone applauded. I bowed my head and walked proudly back to my desk.

"That was the greatest speech I ever heard," said one of the boys.

"You had great raptentious dipardulation," Slim said.

"All right," said the teacher, who gave me an A for the speech.

My high school years were not all fun and games. One day, during a trip to Chicago's Shedd Aquarium, Brick and I were watching the boats on Lake Michigan and listening to the waves that were pounding the concrete pier, unaware of four shadowy figures stalking us. With Brick in front, I climbed a flight of concrete steps and up onto a landing. Suddenly, I was startled by a figure that seemed to have sprung out of nowhere.

"Hey man, give me some money," said the short, thin man wearing a wide-brimmed white hat and a tan overcoat.

At that point I was overtaken with fear—a fear I had never experienced before. I glared at his face—tan and bony, thin nose, yellow protruding teeth and dark and slanted eyes. For the first time in my life, I truly saw the face of evil.

I scanned downward to the man's right hand wrapped around a shiny metal object and my worst fears were realized—the man was holding a gun.

Whether it was instinct, courage, fear or stupidity I don't know, but I uncoiled a right hook to the jaw of my assailant, driving him into the cement wall. Suddenly, I heard a thumping sound and I felt a stinging pain from my head. I dropped to my knees while three other assailants savagely flogged me with metal chains. The thumping became louder and the stinging became unbearable.

They flogged me five or six times, then took off down the steps. I raised myself, wiped the blood from my head and walked to the top of the hill.

"Why didn't you get the hell out of there?" Brick shouted.

"I thought you were next to me," I replied, dazed.

Brick and I walked to the aquarium lobby where a man behind the desk phoned the police. It took twenty minutes before two officers arrived. One of the officers asked me some questions and then drove me to the hospital.

The officer took me to the fourth floor, where I was treated by a young doctor and a middle-aged nurse. Fortunately, my wounds were not too serious—my head was cleaned, stitched and wrapped. I used my head injury as an excuse to skip school the following day. My absence from school spawned rumors spanning from my having been critically ill in a hospital bed in Chicago to having been shot to death. When I returned to school the following Monday, I was an instant celebrity. Several teachers told me how fortunate I was to be alive.

The incident was a learning experience. It should have warned me that I had no peripheral vision—I never saw the assailant until he was directly in front of me and I never saw Brick, who had sprinted away. I was all right as long as someone was in front of me but if they were on either side of me I never saw them.

During this period, my father's business started to dwindle. With the explosion of rock and roll, interest in learning the accordion declined. Even in a predominantly Polish area, no one, especially teens, wanted to become the next Dick Contino or Concertina Millie. It was the guitar, not the accordion, that became the hot musical instrument.

"Forget about the accordion and start to teach guitar," I advised my father. "Rock and roll is the biggest thing—you can make tons of money teaching guitar."

"Rock and roll is junk," he growled. "It won't last long."

During the next few years my father had no students. The only money that we had coming in was from his weekend gigs and my mother's income from her job as a cashier where she earned a whopping $1.25 an hour.

Although I had no job, I tried to do whatever I could to help our financial situation. There were two things I learned from my father: how to box and how to shovel snow. I would offer to shovel the neighborhood residents' walks, that is, for a price. After finishing our massive area, which usually took three or four hours, I'd go around the neighborhood with my father's huge steel shovel on my shoulder, offering my services. The first house I visited was that of an elderly lady who lived in a two-story house with her daughter. Irene was very generous; she usually gave me fifty cents or as much as a dollar, depending on how deep the snow was. On Tuesdays or Wednesdays, I did the grocery shopping for Irene—she'd give me fifty cents and let me keep the change if it wasn't over a dollar.

In June of 1960, a union officer used his influence to land my father a job in construction. Fifty-six years old at that time, my father nearly killed himself his first day on the job. His knees, hips and back were so sore from lifting heavy metal pilings and pushing wheelbarrows of cement that he could barely walk. Despite his age and arthritis, he worked construction for ten years in order to get a pension.

I spent the summers of my teen years playing softball, swimming or just hanging out. As far as my vision problems, there didn't seem to be any—I was having too much fun.

Chapter 5

A Deadly Haze

Unlike Brick, Slim, Richie or any of my buddies, I delayed getting my driver's license. Perhaps it was because I enjoyed riding my bike. However, my biking days came to an abrupt end at a nearby gas station. Moments after I inflated the tires, I found myself lying in the middle of the street after both tires exploded.

I was the last of my friends to get my license. I was frankly afraid of driving. Perhaps it was that, down deep, I knew that there was something worse than I even suspected wrong with my vision—I even worried that I could be incapable of operating a motor vehicle safely. Soon my suspicions grew. From my first time behind the wheel, I felt I was in a tunnel. I had trouble driving at twilight and at night. One dark, glary evening while driving on an unlit street, I was pulled over for weaving. While my friends enjoyed driving, I found it to be stressful. My father often yelled at me for not looking far enough ahead when approaching intersections. Little did I realize that my visual field was restricted.

I told him I had some trouble driving at night.

"My son is night blind," my father told one of his friends.

That was the first time I had heard the term *night blind*.

One evening around twilight, I noticed a light brownish haze near the living room window. At first, I thought it was the faint sunlight reflecting against the floating dust or my father's lingering cigar smoke.

"We'll have to have your eyes checked out again," my father said.

He never followed up on the eye exam and I really didn't pay attention to that haze again, not until years later, when a thicker and much darker version of that haze invaded the edges of my vision. Little did I know that the deadly haze I discovered at age seventeen marked the beginning of the end of my sight.

Brick's older brother Don, who drove a white convertible, allowed Brick to drive several of his "junkers" (provided he could get them in working order). Slim usually picked me up in his father's car. We cruised around Mitchell Street and down Wisconsin Avenue. Because of my visual problems, night blindness in particular, I avoided driving my dad's big yellow car.

We cruised busy Wisconsin Avenue with one of the older guys in the neighborhood. He had his own car, a souped-up brown and orange convertible. He'd stop for every girl, then keep driving. Cruising was not expensive. There was no problem with the price of gas at that time. A few dollars' worth usually provided enough fuel for an entire week of cruising.

Our neighborhood was undergoing subtle changes. Loud, dirty gas busses replaced quiet electric trolley cars. The drugstore, where we hung out buying sodas, sundaes and comic books and where I had many a stitch removed by the pharmacist, became a television repair shop. The place we bought our Christmas trees became a trailer park and the butcher shop where we purchased steaks, chops, chicken and ground beef for our New Year's Eve sandwiches closed.

The vacant lot across from my house was transformed into a large apartment building. When the bulldozers destroyed the wildflowers, grass and sod, they also destroyed a part of my childhood. I had spent many hours in that field playing cowboys, army and football and catching butterflies, grasshoppers and bees. I caught my first blue Monarch, the prize of all butterflies, while it unsuspectingly sat on a yellow dandelion in that field. Before its completion, Slim and I climbed to the second story of the building and spent our evenings laying on the wooden floor, talking and looking up into the night sky.

The gravel lot down the block with the birch trees and the monkey bars where we played softball was turned into a green asphalt playground. The middle tree that separated right and left field and the white birches I had climbed and proudly engraved with my signature were cut down. Many houses along 20th Street in back of the lot were demolished. The large field where I first fired my air rifle, caught spiders and picked pumpkins was turned into an office building. In order to widen streets like Lincoln Avenue, trees and bushes were uprooted and replaced by large slabs of concrete. The creeks where we had caught crayfish became cement drainage ditches.

The faces in the neighborhood also changed. The older Polish residents died while the others moved southwest or to the surrounding suburbs. It seemed that every house on the old block was for sale. Even my old South Division High School was demolished and a new school was built.

The rise of television resulted in the demise of the neighborhood movie houses. The first casualty of that new medium was the Pearl, where I had spent many a Sunday afternoon watching those cowboy movies I adored. Like dominoes, they all fell. And meanwhile, small incidents seemed to indicate that my sight was growing worse.

* * *

Ever since I read my first comic book, my dream was to become a cartoonist. I thought I'd better get a degree of some kind, just in case something happened to prevent me from following my real ambition. What could possibly happen, though? Even if I lost my right arm, I could still draw with the left. Even if I lost both arms, I could still draw with my feet. Even if I lost both arms and both legs, I could still draw with a pen in my teeth. The only thing that could prevent me from my dream would be something like completely losing my vision and I told myself over and over that that couldn't possibly happen.

During my second semester at the University of Wisconsin-Milwaukee (UWM), something happened—something that should have alerted me. Moments after stepping from the glary, snowy January sunlight into the dark student union foyer, I walked into someone. At first, I thought nothing of it. Students were perpetually bumping into each other, racing to their classes in buildings scattered throughout the large campus. I stood for awhile, waited for my eyes to clear and noticed something that took me by surprise. It wasn't merely another student that I had bumped into, but a young lady standing beside a large German Shepherd with what appeared to be a leather contraption strapped under its belly. I immediately apologized.

"Oh, that's all right," she laughed. "That happens all the time."

Her attitude puzzled me. I wondered how someone like her, a young girl afflicted with blindness, could be so upbeat? At that time, I didn't know any blind people. I couldn't imagine what it would be like being blind; having to depend on some dog with that contraption strapped underneath its belly.

When I returned for the fall semester I was notified that I had lost my student deferment (2-S) and might be eligible for the army draft. *They can't draft me if I'm in school*, I thought. On July 1, I reported to the army induction center for a draft physical and, despite not being able to read the third line on the eye chart, lacking depth perception, being colorblind and having tunnel vision, I passed. In November I received a notice that I was to report to the army induction center on December 3 and to bring enough clothes for three days—the letter was signed by Lyndon Baines Johnson, President of the United States. Burning my draft card, fleeing to Canada or breaking my legs did not appeal to me. Fortunately, I was reclassified 2-S and was spared a trip to Vietnam.

One April, six of us piled into a friend's car for our second annual Easter break trip to Daytona. We all took turns driving; that is, everyone but me. Not that I wanted to but I still felt slighted.

"I can drive in the daytime," I said.

"No thanks," my friend replied. I knew he felt that I had vision issues.

What really stood out on that trip were my light-to-dark adaptation problems. I headed back to the room to shower after my morning swim. It took a while for my eyes to clear after entering the building. What bothered me was that some of my other friends also needed glasses. In fact, one friend never went into the water without his contact lenses for fear of not finding his way back to shore. Yet, when wearing his glasses or contacts, I could tell his vision was better than mine.

At UWM, I enrolled in a poetry writing course. It wasn't that I was really interested in poetry or writing but I needed an easy A to boost my sagging grade point average. I never thought much of my writing but apparently the professor did. He was so impressed with my work that he invited me to read alongside him at an eastside coffee house frequented by intellectuals and hippies.

At the end of the semester, I turned in thirty poems in a manila folder. On the cover of the folder, I drew a caricature of my professor surrounded by an assortment of hippie types; above his head were flies. My writing earned me an A. However, the professor was not so generous in his comments about my drawing; "Your writing is superior to your artwork," he wrote.

In February of that year, I attended a reading featuring San Francisco beat poet Allen Ginsberg on the second floor of the UWM student union. The entire floor erupted when Ginsberg, all decked out in a black kimono and sucking on a joint, made his grand entrance. He slowly walked to the podium, stopped to take one last drag and then flipped the joint to the carpet. My poetry professor, following behind like a puppy dog, pounced on the discarded reefer, carefully extinguished it and slipped it into his coat pocket. After the reading, we gathered at my professor's house to hear Ginsberg read from his 1955 masterpiece, *Howl*. At the invitation of Ginsberg himself, several of us stood up in that pot-filled room and read some of our poems—I read three of my short masterpieces. The next time I saw my professor, he was wearing a peculiar medallion—a shellacked steak bone from the food he had served Ginsberg at the party. I'm sure he had Ginsberg's discarded joint bronzed and made into a paperweight.

During that period, I freelanced as a cartoonist for *The UWM Post* and became the head illustrator for campus rival *Crossroads*—later, I illustrated and wrote articles for the Vietnam veteran's newspaper, *The Honey Bucket*.

In order to improve my cartoons, I took a basic drawing course, sketching nude models. For some reason, I had trouble sketching the entire figure. If I started from the head, the lower body was disproportional and vice versa. It didn't occur to me that my restricted visual field prevented me from seeing the entire body.

On December 3, 1970, we had a party at a restaurant. My date was a nineteen-year-old cutie I had met at a UWM frat party. I had a date but my best friend Dale didn't, so I called a girl I knew who fixed him up with Donna Gilewski, a teacher who had recently moved to Milwaukee from Grand Rapids, Michigan.

The following evening, with Dale's permission, I called his date, Donna. She told me she was a kindergarten teacher at Sacred Heart Catholic grade school on Wells Street.

She informed me that she wouldn't go out with me because I was a stranger.

"After we go out, we will not be strangers," I said. "Just think, one date with me could change your whole life. We could even get married."

We had our first date—my next-door neighbor and buddy and his future wife doubled with us. It was the first snowfall of the year and I cautiously drove my father's car to Donna's small apartment. My friends sat in the car while I entered the apartment building. I knocked twice before she opened the door.

"It's you," she said laughing.

"Who did you think it was?"

"The other guy at your table."

I drove to nearby Whitnall Park where we hiked around a small lake. We ended the evening at Pepi's restaurant, a favorite hangout of mine since high school.

On Donna's twenty-fourth birthday, two days after our first date, I gave her the first of many hand-drawn cards. We went to the movies and on hikes in the Whitnall Park area. After each date, we'd end up at Pepi's, a tradition we maintained until its closing.

It took only five or six dates to realize that I was in love with Donna. I wanted to get married but did not have a real job. At that time I was a paid cartoonist for *The UWM Post* and *Crossroads*.

On January 6, while on my way to Donna's apartment, I was involved in an auto accident. While turning left on Highway 24, I collided with an oncoming car. I told myself my failure to see the car was caused by the snowbank on the median. Three months later, while turning onto the expressway during a rainstorm, I plowed into an oncoming car. Once again I made excuses: it must have been the weather that caused the accident. Two months later, I had a collision with a car crossing an intersection on a side street. That's it—that would be my last accident, I vowed. From then on, I would be extra cautious.

"You have to pay attention," lectured my father.

In July of 1970, I bumped into an old friend who had played on our intermural baseball team.

Impressively dressed in a suit and tie and driving a white Milwaukee County car, he told me that he was a social worker. He encouraged me to take the social worker test.

"Just study the welfare statutes and you'll be all set," he said.

In September, I took the test. One month later I received a letter stating that I had scored in the top twenty and would be placed on a waiting list. A year and a half later I was hired as a temporary Milwaukee County social worker and placed at The Infirmary, a large old brick building on the Milwaukee County grounds in Wauwatosa. The Infirmary, once the county nursing home, housed the indigent elderly, many of whom were alcoholics. I would remain in that position until the return of the woman for whom I was temping, who was on a pregnancy leave. My supervisor was a dapper, silver-haired man who spoke with a slight southern drawl. I was assigned a desk in a large office with a chain-smoking woman in her late fifties.

At The Infirmary, my main duties were to visit the residents and monitor their social security checks.

On June 19, 1972, I became a permanent Milwaukee County employee and reported for training to the first floor of the Welfare building on 12th and Vliet Street.

I was one of three from our group who were placed at the old Muirdale building. Located on the beautiful Milwaukee County grounds in Wauwatosa, Muirdale had once been a tuberculosis sanitarium.

In January we were told by our union that we were to participate in a work stoppage. My colleague Doug and I paraded around the Muirdale lot in sub-zero weather carrying crude cardboard signs taped to wooden poles. Those who crossed the picket lines were threatened and greeted with chants of "Scab" and "Union Breaker." Several of the unit supervisors found their cars decorated with eggs and some even had their tires slashed and windows broken. Doug and I usually picketed for an hour, then retreated to a pancake house for breakfast. The contract was settled in four days and we reluctantly returned to Muirdale.

During the winter, I had difficulty going from the bright, snow-covered outside to the dimly-lit hallway; twice I tripped at the base of the stairwell. Later, I became familiar with the hallway stairs and had little difficulty negotiating them.

I wasn't happy at Muirdale. Ever since my playground days, I had yearned to work with children, so in October I was allowed to put in for a transfer to Youth Services in Child Protection.

In November, I purchased my first automobile, a purple compact car. Proudly, I crowded three friends into the $2000 box on wheels for a test run around 5:30 P.M.—twilight, which caused me problems. Turning onto the freeway, I was nearly sideswiped by a car to my right. Although I avoided that accident, there would be plenty more to follow.

The next summer, Donna and I were married. We spent the night at my house, then drove to Kanora, Canada for our honeymoon and stayed in a log cabin above the Lake of the Woods. Our days were spent hiking through the dense forest and climbing bluffs above the cabin. At night, we'd sit on the pier where we'd look at the stars while listening to the water splashing the shore.

It was wonderful. We were so happy; we hadn't a care in the world.

"Everything is going so well," I told Donna.

Little did I realize that in just a few years, the most miserable period of my entire life would begin.

Chapter 6

The Perverse Is the Norm

In March of 1973, I became a Child Protective Services caseworker at the Welfare Center. My mission was to rescue all the abused children in Milwaukee County.

A wide stairway, an escalator and two elevators allowed the workers to freely navigate the three-story building that had once housed a department store.

"Hey, Phil," a male voice called as I walked into Room 320. I glanced to my left and saw a large figure standing at one of the desks.

"What are you doing here?" Jack, a fellow UWM grad, asked while extending his large hand.

"I took the test like you said and here I am. I'm going into child protecting."

"Do you have a supervisor?"

"Not yet."

Scanning the large room, I zoomed in on an attractive lady dressed in a gray pantsuit and a white blouse at the east wall, talking with two men. She turned and quickly walked toward me with one of the men trailing behind her. She introduced herself as Eleanor, the section head of Child Protective Services.

As she spoke, I was fixated on her large brown eyes. We shook hands; she then introduced me to the man who had followed her—my unit supervisor, a short, thin man with brown hair.

I trailed him to his cubicle along the east wall of the large room. After fifteen minutes of extraneous information, my supervisor took me to my new workstation directly across the aisle from his cubicle. Speaking quietly, he introduced me to my state-of-the-art equipment: a small plastic desk calendar, a metal wastebasket and a gray plastic phone.

At 11:00 A.M., we all got together for the weekly staff meeting. One man dominated the meeting. This caseworker spoke about his many experiences dealing with sexual abuse and various types of perversion. He paused briefly at one point to light a cigarette, then continued with his ramblings.

"In child protection, the perverse is the norm," he told me.

At that meeting, he reminisced about a case involving an army service officer who taught his two young boys and daughter about sex by masturbating in front of them.

"When in court, he told the judge, 'I was only trying to enlighten my children as to the normal sexual practices in other cultures.'" That was his defense.

At the weekly meetings, I found that my colleagues were an outspoken, competent and experienced group of social workers.

One night, Donna and I attended a party at a coworker's newly purchased duplex located on the northwest side of Milwaukee. At that point my vision was clouded but with Donna's assistance, I managed to circulate; she stood behind me, grabbed my shoulders as if they were a steering wheel and maneuvered me around furniture, people and other obstacles like trays of food and alcohol.

On my signal, we'd stop to chat with the other workers in my unit. I introduced Donna to Carly, a young woman seated on a couch sipping a beer. I told her about how excited I was and solicited her advice about one of my cases.

"At parties we don't talk shop," Carly said.

However, that apparently didn't apply to the caseworker who usually dominated our meetings, who rambled on and on in lurid detail about his sexual abuse cases.

Carly also told me that no one in child protection lasted more than five years—she was in her fourth year and never made the fifth; one month after the party, she took a medical leave and when she returned, she was transferred into another area.

One of the more interesting protective workers in my unit was slightly older than the rest of us. He wore the same clothes every day: a tight brown t-shirt, a pair of flared jeans and brown sandals. He was an ex-Catholic priest who went into social work. He had made the transition from a Catholic priest to conservative suit-and-tie company man and was married with children.

On my second day, I accompanied Julie, another young caseworker, on an abuse referral involving a nineteen-year-old mother. Staying as close to my colleague as I could, I followed her into an old apartment building near the Marquette University campus. *Shit*, I thought, *I can't see anything in this dark hallway.* What was I to do? If I put my hand on her back or shoulder, she'd discover my visual deficiencies, or worse, accuse me of groping her. I tried making small talk like: "What is the room number?" "Is this the right apartment?" and "Isn't it hot in here?"

I almost gave my vision problems away by saying, "Boy, it's sure dark in here."

Touching the wall with my right hand and listening to her footsteps, I managed to navigate the dark hallway without bumping into her.

"Did you find the apartment?" I kept asking.

Halfway down the hallway she stopped. "This is it," she said.

I rotated my eyes back and forth, trying to see more clearly. Finally I managed to spot a red light above the exit door and was able to make my way.

Julie rang the doorbell three times, after which a young lady opened the door.

"We're from protective services and we'd like to talk with you," Julie said.

The woman slipped off the door chain and let us in. Despite not being able to see clearly, I managed to step carefully into the apartment without knocking anyone or anything over.

We introduced ourselves and told the young mother about the referral which alleged that the woman's boyfriend had not only beaten her child but had burned the child's feet by holding them over a hot stove.

"Can we see the baby?" Julie asked.

While the woman walked into the bedroom, I rolled my eyes around hoping my eyes would adjust to the dimly lit apartment.

The young woman returned with her little girl, wrapped in a yellow blanket, and placed her on the couch.

"Look at this, Phil," Julie said. "Look at the feet."

I squinted and strained my eyes but saw neither bruises nor burns. In fact, I strained to even make out the features of the child.

"Yeah," I responded, pretending to have seen the markings.

The woman also told us that her boyfriend had given the baby a quarter capsule of LSD. Julie wrapped the baby in the blanket and we took her to Children's Hospital. That was my first experience of what we called "child snatching."

One month later, I was involved in a skirmish with a client that could have cost me my job. The abuse referral regarded a student from a relatively new school located on the southwest side of Milwaukee. I spoke briefly with the principal who explained the reason for the referral; her stepfather had beaten her for engaging in some sexual activity on the lawn near the school.

He excused himself to get the girl while I sat behind his desk. That was the first time that I had sat behind a principal's desk or had been in a principal's office without being disciplined. The principal brought the girl and again excused himself. She was tall and thin with long brown hair. She spoke quietly and was sobbing. She waited for the principal to leave and leaned toward me. "Look at this," she sobbed, pulling back her hair. "My stepfather did this to me."

From what I could see, the sides of her face were scratched and bruised. Her left eye was swollen and blackened. She looked at me with tears streaming down her cheeks. "My stepfather is a drunk and he always beats me."

She told me about the incident on the lawn and how her younger stepbrother informed on her. She warned me about talking to her father—how mean he was and how, in a drunken rage, he might attack me.

As an inexperienced worker, I made the fatal mistake of driving to her house with an attitude. All I could think of were the bruises on the girl's face. They rekindled memories of my own childhood and my father. I thought about the bruises on my mother. I thought about the time my father sent my sister Tana to school with a swollen black eye—she was the same age as this girl.

By the time I reached the girl's house, I was all worked up, ready to attack that drunken son of a bitch.

The girl's mother, a short, thin woman who appeared much older than the thirty-eight years documented in my referral, met me at the door and led me into the living room. Thanks to the bright sunlight and a large bay window, I had no problem navigating to a small sofa.

Speaking softly and measuring her words, the woman denied that her husband was alcoholic or abusive.

"My daughter is always getting into trouble. She drinks, swears and stays out all night." She also told of how the girl was always getting into trouble, especially with boys, and how difficult it was for her stepfather to deal with her.

About twenty minutes later, a short man wearing a white T-shirt came into the room. I stood up and politely introduced myself. As her stepfather spoke I noticed his speech was slurred; the cigarette draped over the right side of his mouth shook with each word.

"My stepdaughter deserved to be disciplined, because she let some boy violate her on the school lawn!" he said.

At first, I tried to be diplomatic. "Listen, you shouldn't hit your daughter—her face is all bruised."

"There were at least twenty kids watching that little whore," he growled.

"I can understand how you feel but you shouldn't beat up a child."

"What the hell do you know about kids?"

Angry as I was, I tried to be tactful with him, although I knew that being subtle with a man like that was nearly impossible.

"I know that hitting a kid is bad, especially a fifteen-year-old."

"What the hell does an asshole like you know? I've got eight kids. How many kids do you have?"

Flippantly, I reeled out the standard answer that we unmarried social workers used: "I have twenty-one children on my caseload."

Again, he called me an asshole. This time however, he raised his right arm and lunged at me. Instinctively, I grabbed his arm and spun him around. Reverting back to my wrestling days, I bear-hugged him and body slammed him to the living room floor. "YOU DO THAT AGAIN," I shouted, kneeling over him, "AND I'LL BREAK YOUR ARM!"

My God, I thought, raising my head. I glanced over to see his stunned wife grabbing the two young children. *What am I doing?* I thought. *I could get fired for this.*

I helped the shaken man to his feet and gently sat him on the couch.

The next morning, I expected to be called in for physical abuse to a client but neither the girl's stepfather nor his wife filed a complaint. A week later, I made a follow-up visit. Not only was the father sober, but also polite. His stepdaughter, dressed in jeans and a gray sweatshirt, sat on the couch and lit a cigarette. "We've straightened everything out," she said. "We're all going camping." *How about that*, I thought.

Later that week, I met with the girl at a fast-food restaurant near her school. I bought her one of those shakes made from dissolvable plastic and gave her a fatherly sermon.

"You're fifteen, so I'm not going to give you a lecture on sex," I said softly.

She looked at me wide-eyed.

"If you're going to...uh," I continued.

"Yes?"

"Uh, engage in some type of..."

"Yes?" she snickered.

"You know what I'm trying to say."

"I do?"

"If you're going to do it, and I don't condone doing it, but if you're going to do it, be sure to use contraception and don't do it in front of an audience."

In July, I received a referral for a prostitute living in a trailer park in the far southern region of Milwaukee County. The referral stated that she was neglecting her two children, a nine-year-old boy and a six-year-old girl. While the mother was out all night, the boy was alleged to be wandering around the trailer camp starting fires.

"She works at a bar in South Milwaukee and has been known to bring men into the trailer while the children are around," her probation officer told me.

On a hot July afternoon, I met with the woman outside her trailer. It was evident by her appearance—thin and haggard—that the thirty-five-year-old Robin had been around the block a few times.

"I have to work second shift but I never leave the children alone," she said. She spoke slowly and deliberately. "My son is a problem. He may have started a fire once, that's all." She said the neighbors hated her and her sister, who babysat the children when she was at work.

The woman led me into the trailer and to a small table next to the stove. The trailer was perfect for me; well-lit and small enough for me to navigate without getting lost.

She brought out the two children who shared a bedroom next to the kitchen. The boy was thin with light brown hair and green eyes. He was wearing a clean T-shirt, a clean pair of jeans and black and white sneakers—he certainly did not look neglected. While we talked, he made noises and rolled around on the floor.

Robin said the children had no friends— that the neighbors looked down on her and the children.

"He plays with my boyfriend when he comes over," she said.

"What's up?" asked a high-pitched, perky voice from behind my left shoulder.

"This is my sister," Robin said.

I stood up, squinted and extended my right hand. "I'm Phil DiMeo."

"He's from the welfare department," Robin said.

From what I could see, she was a taller, younger and sexier version of her older sister. I thought she looked to be about twenty, with long straight brown hair and large dark eyes. She was wearing a tight-fitting halter top and cutoffs that looked as if they had been spray painted on her thighs.

"Is this a private party or can I join you?" she asked.

She pulled out a chair and sat to my left.

"I'll have a beer," she said to Robin who was at the stove pouring coffee.

"I understand that you baby-sit the children while Robin is at work?" I asked.

She slid her chair toward me and leaned in. "Whenever I can."

Robin placed a large cup of coffee to my right and then sat down.

"So you're from the welfare department?" her sister asked.

"Yes."

"Can you get me anything?"

"Like what?"

"Money, a house, a rich man?"

"It's about my son—some people down the block complained about my boyfriend," Robin said. Robin then told her sister to take the children outside.

The following week I made an announced visit to the trailer. I spoke briefly with Robin, but it was her son I wanted to see.

"I have something for you," I said.

His eyes lit up as I pulled one of my footballs from the hatchback and gave it to him.

I took him to a small grassy area and demonstrated how to grip the ball. We played catch for about twenty minutes.

When I returned the following week, Robin's son had found a friend to play catch with—a week later it seemed that every boy in the trailer park was playing football with him.

On my third visit, I met one of Robin's male friends. Later, I was informed by several of the neighbors that the friend wasn't the only "john" to frequent the trailer.

"Robin and that whore sister have plenty of gang bangs. That trailer is a goddam whorehouse," said one of the ladies.

I continued my weekly visits to the trailer, much to the delight of Robin's son. However, in late September Robin was arrested for pandering and I was forced to place the children in receiving homes—the case was transferred to foster care.

As a caseworker I learned many things. The most important was to verify the referral. Many of the abuse referrals were bogus. Mrs. Jones would accuse Mrs. Smith of child abuse because she didn't like Mrs. Smith or because Mrs. Smith's dog pooped all over Mrs. Jones's sidewalk.

In September, I received a referral that Gayle Mason had been neglecting her three small children. Gayle lived on the first floor of an old duplex in the heart of the inner city. The referral stated that the house was cluttered with garbage and infested with roaches. All decked out in my blue polyester sportcoat and blue-and-white striped polyester flares with cuffs, I met with Gayle in the living room. "Please have a seat," she said politely. I placed my Milwaukee County briefcase on the floor and sat on her soft couch.

While we spoke, one of her sons was throwing his shoe against the wall.

"What are you doing?" I asked.

"Killin' bugs."

I turned to the wall and squinted, but saw nothing.

I didn't think much about the house and the bugs until that evening, when Donna screamed loudly from the bathroom. There it was, our souvenir from Mrs. Mason: a large, hideous brown roach crawling along the sink basin. From that time on, I never sat on a client's couch and never wore cuffed pants.

In another case, the father was a part-time truck driver while the mother worked at the mall. The referral, which came from the nurse at the children's school, stated that the father, Arthur Sims, abused his wife and two children, an eleven-year-old boy and a nine-year-old girl.

It was 3:00 P.M. when I met with the school principal, a tall middle-aged man. He stunned me by offering me a swig of brandy from a bottle he kept in his desk drawer.

"I'm on the wagon," I replied.

He directed me to the office of the nurse who had initiated the referral. She felt that the father was abusing the little girl but wasn't sure about the boy.

"I have not seen bruises on him, but the little girl came to school with bruises on her back, buttocks and legs."

The Sims lived in a small ranch house about three blocks from the school. The wife met me at the doorway and led me through the small living room into the kitchen. The bright afternoon sun beaming through the kitchen and living room windows provided adequate light for me to survey the area—clean and orderly, no rats, roaches or feces.

Mrs. Sims had light brown wavy hair and wore glasses. She told me her husband was at work and the children were in the yard. She studied me for a few moments and then began talking freely about her husband.

"Arthur frequently hits me and our daughter. He always hits her, but not our son; he never hits him."

"Does he do anything else to your daughter?"

She paused and glanced toward the door. "Not that I know of."

Unlike some of the other abused women I met, Barbara Sims seemed assertive and did not appear to fear her husband; nevertheless, she made it clear that she wanted him in jail.

She called her daughter from the backyard and the three of us went into a bedroom.

Mrs. Sims placed her daughter on her lap while I sat in a chair at the foot of the bed. I started my interview by asking the little girl about her friends, favorite activities and about school. Mrs. Sims broke in, "Tell Mr. DiMeo about your father and how he hits you."

The girl looked at me wide-eyed.

"Come on," whispered Mrs. Sims.

"He hits me sometimes."

Mrs. Sims placed the girl on the bed and gently unbuttoned her yellow blouse.

"Look at this," she said.

Fortunately, the light in the bedroom was adequate for me to see; there were some bruises and scratches on the girl's arms and chest.

I took a deep breath. "When did this happen?"

"Two days ago. The nurse sent her home and we took her to the hospital. Arthur told the doctor that she fell."

The following morning Mrs. Sims, her daughter and I met with the district attorney. With her daughter on her lap, she told him about her husband's physical abuse, then led her over to him. As she had done at my first interview, Mrs. Sims unbuttoned her daughter's blouse and pointed to the marks, still visible on the little girl's chest and arms.

The DA quickly scanned the girl, then with Mrs. Sims's approval, called for a photographer.

The DA and I sat across from each other as a tall middle-aged woman led the girl and her mother to a private room. He assured me that the testimonies of the teachers and nurses, along with that of Mrs. Sims, would be enough to put her husband away.

All primed for a contentious hearing, I returned to the courthouse two weeks later only to learn that a deal between the defense attorney and the DA had been struck. Mr. Sims would remain in the home, attend family therapy and counseling. I was granted an order of supervision for a six-week period.

My weekly visits were unannounced and were on different days and at different times. During that period, Mr. Sims obeyed the order. He attended all the counseling sessions and did not assault Mrs. Sims or his daughter. If they were giving out awards for fatherhood, he would have won, at least for those six weeks.

After the six weeks, however, things reverted back to where they were before my intervention. Mr. Sims resumed his physical abuse and threatened to kill his wife; he was eventually charged with child abuse and jailed.

The next April, I was assigned the Tate case and met with the complainant, June Tate, in the kitchen of an old southside duplex. June was short, frail and drawn and like many abused women I met, appeared older than the thirty-three years stated in the referral. She told me her husband, Carl, a heroin addict, frequently beat her and ordered her and her two children, a thirteen-year-old daughter whom he had molested and a six-year-old son, to watch while he stood on the kitchen table masturbating.

She rolled up her sleeves to show me her pale, thin arms—they were covered with welts and bruises. "He did this with a frying pan," she whispered.

June told me about his guns: two rifles and a handgun that he kept in the attic. "He's held a loaded rifle at my head and threatened to kill me and the children," she said.

Several days later, I met with Carl, a short, thin man with black hair, a pale complexion and piercing black eyes. His speech, soft and slow, held a slight southern accent.

I told him we had an abuse referral. He glared, raised his voice and demanded, "Who made it?"

"I'm not allowed to reveal that information," I replied.

"Was it my wife?"

I told him the referral was anonymous. I didn't want June beaten after I left.

He stared stoically while I listed the specific allegations of abuse and masturbation on the kitchen table.

"How I conduct my family business is my business, not the government's, the neighbors', the school's or yours."

Again, he demanded to know where the referral came from and again I insisted that it was anonymous.

I left the house with a creepy feeling. Not even going into the worst part of the city gave me that uneasy feeling that I felt after my brief meeting with Carl.

At around 2:00 A.M. the following morning, I received a frightening phone call.

"The next time I see you, I'm going to put a bullet hole right through your head," said a voice in a cold menacing whisper. To say that I was scared was an understatement.

Apparently, Carl had found my name in the phone book. The next day I told my supervisor about the call and he immediately called the police. I thought the threatening caller was Carl Tate, I told the officer, but I couldn't prove it. All I knew was that I wouldn't allow myself to be intimidated by Tate, even if it meant bodily harm or worse.

One week later, I nervously walked the narrow sidewalk between the Tate house and the adjacent duplex. I waited outside until my eyes adjusted before walking into the shadows.

Mrs. Tate greeted me at the door and assured me that her husband was not home. Again, she warned me about his gun collection, one of which was an assault rifle. I envisioned Mr. Tate, like Lee Harvey Oswald, up at the attic window, perched in a chair with a rifle propped on the window-sill, looking into a scope with my head in the crosshairs.

I pleaded with Mrs. Tate to divorce her abusive husband and change her residence, but her powerlessness and dependency on her husband prevented her from taking such action.

Two weeks later, I received a call from the hospital where Mrs. Tate was in the Intensive Care Unit. Her daughter had told the police that Mr. Tate had beaten her mother with a frying pan. The Sheriff's Department had issued a warrant for his arrest but he apparently had fled south. When I saw her, Mrs. Tate was lying in a hospital bed with tubes inserted into every part of her body— that's when she made the decision to divorce her husband.

Our section head, Eleanor, seeking recognition for her department, contacted *The Milwaukee Journal* about the Tate case, which she referred to as one of many great success stories in Child Protective Services. Several weeks later, Mrs. Tate and I met with a reporter and photographer. The photographer circled the kitchen snapping pictures while Mrs. Tate and I sat pretending to talk.

Her story appeared in the May 6 Sunday supplement of *The Milwaukee Journal*. Mrs. Tate was referred to as Jane. There was a photograph of her sitting at her kitchen table with her back to the camera talking to me. The Tate case made me an instant celebrity and, for a brief period, I was one of our section head's darlings.

By that point I had settled into a routine at Child Protective Services—arriving before 8:00 A.M., returning phone messages and completing paperwork. My fieldwork was usually in the afternoon. With rare exceptions, most home visits were unannounced.

When I received a referral on the Diaz case, I didn't know what to expect. Mr. Diaz was alleged to have been neglecting his two stepchildren; a nine-year-old girl and a seven-year-old boy—no specifics. The referral also made mention of animals, but again no specifics.

The Diazes lived on the first floor of an old wooden duplex. At the front, a large old-fashioned porch with five wooden steps extended downward to a narrow walkway followed by six cement steps and a bent pipe railing anchored on the right. Approaching the house, I heard what sounded like a scraping noise coming from the porch. I paused at the first wooden step and squinted. I thought it was a pet scratching. I took a step, stopped and took another step, which put me in the shadow of the overhang.

Unable to spot anything, I continued up the cement steps, the old worn wooden steps and onto the sagging porch. The sound of scratching or scraping caught my attention; again I stopped to listen. Squinting with eyes fixated on the front door, I managed to spot what appeared to be a large gray furry animal directly in front of me. Was it one of those animals mentioned in the referral? For several minutes I stood listening while I waited for my eyes to clear.

When things came into focus, I discovered my gray furry friend was neither the family dog nor an alley cat, but a large rat. I could barely make out the eyes and mouth but there was no mistaking that long obtrusive tail—like a thin whip, coiled and ready to strike.

Quickly, I retreated down the steps to the walkway, which I followed around to the backyard. I heard a series of loud, menacing growls as I approached the old, rotted wooden gate. Now what? A pet wolf, a bear or a lion?

Safely behind the gate, I spotted a large German Shepherd tethered to a metal pole barking furiously and trying to pull loose.

"Who is it?" asked a woman's voice.

"May I come in?" I replied.

A petite woman approached me, standing on the other side of the gate. She inquired as to who I was and why I was in her backyard. I identified myself and handed her my official Milwaukee County Protective Services ID card.

She unlocked the gate and let me in. As we stood by the gate, the German Shepherd was growling and sizing me up.

"That's a beautiful dog," I commented. "Mind if I pet him?"

"He don't take to strangers," she warned.

I assured her that I had a way with dogs. "If you show no fear and let them know who's the boss, they will not hurt you," I said.

"That's what they say."

I knew that and she knew that, but more importantly, did the dog know that? Ever so cautiously, I approached the angry beast that was barking and trying to pull loose. The lady and a girl of about nine or ten stood wide-eyed awaiting my next move.

Slowly, I turned toward the dog, furiously growling and beating his tail against the pole. Twice, he sprung forward, trying to free himself. The pole shimmied and shook—ready to be uprooted from its cement base.

I told myself, *It's too late to stop now.*

Firmly, I raised my right hand and commanded him to sit. He continued barking and pulling. Again, I commanded him to sit. He just looked at me—didn't know what to make of me. On the third command, he sat. I stroked him under the chin, then reached out, snapped my fingers and commanded him to shake. He lifted his left paw and I gently clasped it.

I made small talk with the little girl while the woman went into the house to get her husband, who, according to the girl, was in the basement catching rats.

While we talked, I looked toward the dog, sprawled out on the grass. *What a beautiful animal*, I thought. I wouldn't have minded owning him myself.

About ten minutes later, I heard the door bang open against the house and saw a tall, heavy-set man carrying what to me looked like a broom, a rake or some kind of pole. When I focused in, I discovered it was neither rake nor broom; it was a pitchfork and the sharp metal prongs were penetrating the belly of a large squealing rat. He had actually pitchforked a rat.

If that wasn't bad enough, he carried the pitchforked rat to a cement ash box near the alley, poured gasoline over the bloody animal and set it on fire.

"Look at that sucker burn!" he shouted, clapping his hands.

The spectacle of the man jumping, clapping and shouting at the tormented animal sent chills up my spine—it was one of the most disgusting things I had ever seen. I realized that what I was dealing with was a first-class psycho.

Mr. Diaz took me into the kitchen and offered me a cup of coffee, which I refused.

From his accent, I concluded that he was from somewhere in the south. He informed me that he was born in Indiana and had moved to Alabama.

The kitchen reeked of excrement, probably from the dog or possibly from the Diazes themselves. The floor was littered with cigarette butts, empty cans, garbage and rotted food. The refrigerator, tilted with a broken door, was decorated with maggots.

Mr. Diaz took me on a tour of the house; the other rooms were decorated similarly—dirty, smelly and covered with garbage. Cautiously, I measured my steps so as not to step into anything hidden by a shadow or under a clump of trash. Mr. Diaz saw nothing wrong with the condition of the house or of his two stepchildren, grimy and dressed in filthy clothes.

Charging the Diazes with neglect would be easy—especially after the judge got a look at Mr. Diaz, I suspected. I imagined Mr. Diaz staggering into court with a can of beer in one hand and a bottle of whiskey in the other. Naturally, he'd be filthy and unshaven and wearing a torn, stained T-shirt while the wife and children would be dressed in rags covered with maggots and feces.

Brimming with impudence, I swaggered into the courthouse later in the month. A neatly dressed man caught my attention as I approached the bench. He looked vaguely familiar but I couldn't place him. Was he a lawyer I had dealt with, a judge or perhaps another social worker? Then it came to me—it was Mr. Diaz, clean-shaven and decked out in a white shirt, a dark tie and wearing a gray polyester suit with wide lapels. He looked as if he had just stepped out of a catalog. *Hell, he's dressed better than me*, I thought.

Behind him stood a young lady in a tan suit who presented herself as the guardian ad litem. To her left were Mrs. Diaz and the children—looking very stylish.

It didn't take a prophet to predict where this was going. They would contest my neglect case and strike a compromise, which they did. I was granted an order of supervision which stipulated that I was to visit the Diazes for six more weeks.

Our homemaking crew was assigned the task of cleaning that filthy home. Three times a week, they reluctantly visited the Diazes where they emptied trash and scrubbed the walls and floors. An exterminator was hired to destroy the rats, much to the disappointment of Mr. Diaz.

After six weeks, the Diaz house appeared fit for human habitation. During my visitation, the Diazes honored the order. They were polite and cooperated in every way. Eight weeks after the hearing, I closed out the Diaz case. Unfortunately, I heard later that the house again fell into disrepair and the Diazes were referred to our department again, but to a different agent.

As I gained experience, I became familiar with the areas I frequented and the types of individuals with whom I had to deal. I had no problems working the southside where I had lived and I soon became familiar with the inner city. Usually, I was assigned abuse cases rather than neglect cases, which was okay with me. My supervisor honored my requests: he assigned me the tough abuse cases—he referred to me as his most aggressive worker, which did not sit well with some of the veteran agents.

I liked my fellow workers but, because of my visual deficiencies, I kept to myself during the workday. However, with Donna as an escort, I did attend parties. During the Christmas season, the parties were usually held at restaurants. The best parties, however, were on the third floor of the Welfare building during the holidays.

Chapter 7

The Beginning of the End

The saving of abused children, the exposure to committed professionals like doctors, nurses, therapists, the police, judges, court officials and even the parents, motivated and provided me with satisfaction and pride while in child protection. However, my enthusiasm tapered when I began experiencing greater difficulty with light-dark adaptation. Several times I tripped on stairways after leaving dark buildings. Sunglasses cut some of the glare and made the transition from light to dark more manageable. I wore the glasses outside and removed them when entering a building. Sometimes it took five minutes or more standing in a dimly lit hallway before my vision cleared.

At that point, I was perceiving my visual problems to be more than lack of depth perception or lazy eye. One month after transferring into Child Protective Services, I made the mistake of joining several workers for a luncheon at a nearby bar. Moments after entering, I stumbled into tables and chairs before being rescued by one of my coworkers. Like my wife, he grabbed my shoulders and steered me to the area where my unit was seated.

Testifying in court also became a problem. The courthouse was downtown and parking was in a large indoor structure, which meant going from bright sunlight to dark. After entering, I'd sit for several minutes and slowly drive the car up the ramp until I found a spot. Inside, I stopped, removed my dark glasses and, when my eyes were somewhat adjusted, continued. While exiting the Milwaukee County courthouse with a high-profile female attorney, I tumbled down the large, bright concrete steps.

No matter what I did, my problems with light to dark worsened. I tried every type of sunglasses; photo grays, mirrored and ultra-dark wraparounds. Nothing worked. I was constantly removing my glasses when entering a building and putting them on when returning outside.

Fearing that someone would discover my secret, I was a loner. Some of the workers in my unit made comments that I was unfriendly and hostile, because I would not engage in any lunchtime activities. That was okay with me, as long as no one suspected my vision problems.

*   *   *

On January 7, I met with my new supervisor. His attire was simple: a tan short-sleeve shirt, dark brown pants with a thin dark belt. A pair of pale blue eyes sat beneath thick blond eyebrows and his blond hair was short and wavy.

Perhaps it was his appearance or the way he comported himself, I don't know, but I liked him immediately.

He was honest, unpretentious and always backed his workers. He was a man's man.

"I hear you take all the tough cases," he said.

"Actually, the cases are easy but I make them tough," I joked.

He assigned me the Miller case in which a nineteen-year-old alleged that her twenty-eight-year-old husband was abusing their six-month-old daughter.

Another abuse case—*no problem*, I thought; that is until he told me the father was a member of the notorious Outlaws motorcycle gang.

"Do you want me to go with you?" he asked.

"No, I'll be all right," I replied.

The Outlaws had a violent reputation. They were alleged to have beaten, maimed and even killed bystanders along with rival gang members. *I have to be crazy to accept that case*, I thought.

The couple who we were investigating lived in an old southside duplex not too far from my old neighborhood. Wary of being pursued when I left, I parked two blocks from the house.

I stood on the porch for a few minutes, then got up enough courage to rap on the storm door, praying that no one would answer. To my dismay, however, the door opened and a young girl with a soft, high-pitched voice let me inside. After identifying myself, I followed her into the living room where I stood for a few moments waiting for my eyes to clear, then sat on an old, worn couch near the window.

The young woman introduced herself as the mother of the alleged abuse victim.

Speaking softly, I went through the referral and asked her if her husband abused her daughter. She said nothing. It was apparent to me that she was scared, which could mean only one thing: her Outlaw husband was somewhere nearby—that meant big trouble for me.

He was there all right and was what I envisioned a member of the Outlaws to be. Wearing a pair of faded jeans and a dirty white T-shirt to accentuate his large pecs and biceps, the huge Ken Miller thundered into the living room demanding to know who the hell I was and why I was talking to his wife. A politely as I could, I introduced myself and told him about the abuse referral.

"Where the hell did that referral come from?"

"I'm not allowed to disclose that information," I responded, not wanting to implicate his wife, who was sitting across from me and trembling.

"I'll show you," he growled, turning and stomping into the bedroom.

Now what was he up to? Was he going to get a tire iron, a knife or perhaps a gun?

"Take a look," he snarled, dangling a naked baby. "There's not a mark on her."

I gently took the child, placed her on the couch and examined her. *Thank God there are no marks on her*, I thought. "She looks okay to me," I said. I handed the baby to his wife, who took her into the bedroom.

"Listen, I want to know who made the referral!" he demanded.

"I can't tell you that."

"Was it my wife?"

"No—she didn't know anything about this."

"You're not leaving this house until you tell me who made that bullshit referral."

I had to think of something—I wasn't about to implicate his wife. I was still wondering why she claimed the child was beaten when there wasn't a mark on her. I pulled out one of my official Milwaukee County Protective Services cards and scribbled down my section head's work number.

"This woman is my boss. She'll straighten out this mess; she'll tell you everything," I said. Then I got out of there as quickly as I could.

* * *

"Would you like a cup of coffee?" Mrs. James asked from the kitchen stove.

"Oh, no," I replied. I had other things on my mind. The roar of traffic on busy Capitol Drive meant that it was getting near rush hour and that meant it was getting dark and that meant driving home in the dark.

"Stephen is in his room and my husband will be home shortly," she said.

I followed Mrs. James through the living room, careful not to knock anything over. I narrowly missed a lamp. She led me up a flight of stairs, turned left and stopped.

"This is my son's bedroom," she said. "Stephen, are you in there?" she asked. She rapped twice, then opened the door.

Stephen, wearing a clean blue and white striped shirt and blue slacks, was sprawled across the bed playing with a red plastic fire truck.

After Mrs. James left, I pulled up a chair and sat at the foot of the bed. I started the conversation by asking him about school, his friends and then about his stepfather: "Does he ever hit you?"

"I don't think so," he muttered.

As we talked, I scanned the bedroom. On the dresser were various toys; miniature trains, cars, trucks and a large teddy bear; on the floor, more toys and a few candy wrappers.

I asked him about his grandmother, the complainant alleging physical abuse from the stepfather. Stephen told me that he visited his grandmother on weekends and that she always gave him presents; clothes, candy and toys.

Although a bit overweight, Stephen did not appear to be abused or even neglected. There was something else going on.

It was around 6:30 P.M. when Mr. James finally arrived. He had high cheekbones and a bulldog jaw. He spoke slowly and softly—his voice was deep and nasal. When I felt he was somewhat comfortable with me, I brought up the referral alleging abuse

"It's the grandmother," he responded. "She spoils him. She gives him everything. She just spoils him rotten. She bought him a truck and an air gun without my permission. She gives him money and he goes and buys candy."

As he spoke, I looked over to Mrs. James, seated next to her husband.

"What do you think?"

"He never hit Stephen. That referral came from my mother. We find candy wrappers under the covers and on the floor. She gives him money to buy candy." She paused and lit a cigarette. "The other night, I found a half-eaten peanut butter and jelly sandwich under his pillow."

"It's the damn grandmother!" erupted Mr. James.

My follow-up visits revealed no abuse. However, I found the problems with the grandmother had affected the marriage and Stephen's behavior and so I recommended counseling. The James' went to weekly sessions and felt it had been a positive experience, especially for Mr. James. The grandmother, however, made it known that she was an unwilling participant.

One month after my initial visit, my section head told me that I was to participate in a counseling session with the James family at the mental health center. I had no idea what to expect.

When I arrived at the hospital, I was greeted by a camera technician, taken to a large room and seated in a chair across from Mr. and Mrs. James, Stephen and his grandmother.

Damn, I thought, *the whole thing is being taped.* I was surrounded by the sound equipment and dazzling lights, which intensified my vision problems. The psychiatrist entered the room and sat somewhere to the left of me—the bright lights blinded me to the point that I couldn't see much of anything. We waited for instructions from a short, thin man; probably the director who was standing behind one of the lights.

The psychiatrist initiated the discussion by introducing himself and the rest of us. Reading notes from a clipboard, he summarized the problems in the James family. Mrs. James felt that her mother was destroying their marriage and their relationship with Stephen. Mr. James felt that his mother-in-law despised him because he didn't make a lot of money.

"She buys things for Stephen that I can't afford. She's turning my own son against me."

"You mean your stepson," interrupted the grandmother.

"Oh, yes. I was married before."

Mr. James and the grandmother lashed out at each other while I sat blinded by the intense lights.

"What do you think, Mr. DiMeo?" the psychiatrist asked.

"Well, I think the grandmother has had an effect on Stephen's behavior."

"In what way?"

"Uh, she buys him too many things."

"That's what I said," moaned Mr. James.

Two weeks later, my section head called me and told me she had seen the tape.

"You were great," she complimented me.

"Really?"

"Yes. You handled yourself professionally. I'm going to show the tape tomorrow at 11:00."

I invited Donna to the tape showing in the Baldwin Room of The Welfare Building. About fifteen attended the showing of what was titled *The Wicked Grandmother*. The tape was used for training for students and new social workers. Years later, a young lady approached me in the cafeteria and asked if I was the star of *The Wicked Grandmother*.

The more I got to know my boss, the more I loved him. His approach to social work was at odds with traditional social work theory. His attire, his politics and his manner of speech were not exactly in the social worker's guide. His unit meetings were unique. At first the meetings took place in the plywood room across from the escalator and later we fled to a bar where we assigned and discussed cases and consumed their greasy cheeseburgers and beer.

Early one Monday morning, I received a call from a parole officer at the Department of Corrections. According to the officer, my next referral, Laura Clark, had quite a past. There was auto theft, forgery, robbery and drug dealing. I was to meet the officer and two FBI agents at Laura's house. Speaking slowly, the officer laid out her daring plan. With the assistance of the FBI agents, she would arrest Laura—my part was to snatch and place her two young boys in a temporary home.

It was a dangerous but clever strategy. She would keep Laura occupied while I grabbed the kids.

At 3:30 P.M. on the day before Thanksgiving, I drove to the Clark house on North 32nd Street. I circled the block while surveying the area—no officer and no FBI. Anticipating the possibility of needing a quick getaway, I parked my car directly across the street from the house.

I tiptoed into the dark hallway, waited for my eyes to clear, placed my hand on the wall for support and climbed the dirty stairs. At the top, I stopped and then slid my right hand along the wall. At last I felt the door. Not quite sure of my surroundings, I stood still, gathered my thoughts, took a deep breath and waited for my eyes to clear.

That old duplex had the smell of mold, rotted wood and damp, cracked plaster—the familiar smell of poverty.

Was Laura in there or not? I leaned over, cupped my hands and listened; I heard nothing. *Here we go*, I thought—I rapped twice, stopped, rapped another two times, stopped and listened. Was this just another home visit or was I walking into an FBI raid? I was filled with apprehension. I rapped two more times.

"Hold on!" screeched a voice from inside.

I heard what sounded like slippers shuffling across the floor. The door shimmied and swung open. There before me was the silhouette of a woman. Squinting, blinking and trying to focus, I nervously introduced myself.

"Come in," she said, stepping to the left.

For a few seconds I stood waiting for my eyes to clear, then stepped into what appeared to be the kitchen. She pulled out a chair at a table near the window.

"You can sit there," she said.

I explained to her that I had received a referral alleging that she had been involved in illegal activities.

She jerked her head forward and leaned toward me.

"Are you from the police?" she whispered.

"No. I'm a social worker from the Department of Welfare."

"I don't need no welfare."

"I'm from Child Protective Services and my referral alleges that you have been neglecting your children."

She loudly called her children to the room.

Two young boys darted out of the bedroom and stood beside their mother.

"Do they look neglected?" she asked, grabbing the left arm of the nine-year-old.

He peered toward me. He was a handsome, intelligent-looking boy with curious light blue eyes, long wavy blond hair and a slender build.

I extended my right hand and said, "How do you do?" He paused, stared at my hand and then slid his small hand into my palm. I clasped and squeezed. "Come on, give me the grip."

He grimaced, his face turned red and he squeezed hard.

"Great handshake. I love a man with a firm handshake."

He bit his lip and tried to apply more pressure.

Pretending to be in pain, I pulled away and flexed my hand. "You're too strong for me."

He beamed proudly. Laura laughed.

Having broken the ice with the older boy, I looked to my right where the six-year-old stood.

"Come on, you give me the grip, too."

He turned toward his older brother for approval.

"Go ahead."

The younger boy reached out with both hands. Half grimacing, he squeezed tightly.

"That's it, give him the grip!" his brother shouted.

"I give, I give," I said. "You're a strong fellow, just like your brother."

"I'm six years old," he replied.

Like his brother, the younger boy was handsome. He was slender with pale brown eyes, thin lips and long light brown wavy hair. Both boys bore no resemblance to their mother. From what I could tell, they hadn't been physically abused or neglected. Their clothes were old but adequate, unlike some neglected children I had dealt with.

"We're getting ready for Thanksgiving," Laura said. "I have to go out and buy the turkey."

The two boys returned to the bedroom as I sat staring at the door.

I felt stupid. What would I do when the officer and the FBI came? How could I face the boys? Maybe they wouldn't come and I wouldn't have to snatch the boys.

The more I thought about it, the more I convinced myself that the officer wouldn't show up. But I was wrong. Two hard raps on the door alerted me that something was about to happen. Laura pushed away from the table and shuffled to the door. I sat still.

"Who is it?" she shouted.

"It's me," a female voice called.

This is it, I thought. I didn't know what to expect. I didn't think that the officer and the FBI would kick down the door with guns drawn, but I wasn't sure. Maybe she came alone?

Laura opened the door; two large men stomped into the kitchen. The officer stood in the hallway.

The men identified themselves to Laura. Then the officer who had been in the hallway came in. She was petite, with long straight brown hair and large brown eyes. She looked at Laura, who appeared to be quite stunned.

"You violated your parole," scolded the officer.

"I didn't do anything!" shouted Laura. Her loud response drew the two boys back into the room.

"I'm going to have to arrest you," the officer continued.

"What about the boys?"

"Mr. DiMeo will take care of them."

I looked over to where the boys were standing. The older one was glaring at the two men and the younger looked over toward me. He wanted to see what I would do. Would I save his mother or would I let the officer and the men take her away? What I had to do at that point was find a receiving home for the boys and that wouldn't be easy. Politely as I could, I asked Laura if I could use her phone. I didn't know whether she had noticed my vision problems, but she led me to a table in the living room where the phone was located. Unfortunately, in that dark room I couldn't see anything, let alone a black telephone. I slid my hand across the table but wasn't able to locate that elusive phone. Suddenly, I heard a loud thump—before I realized what had happened, I was on all fours, stunned, with the back of my neck throbbing.

"Laura," the officer called from the kitchen. "What have you done?"

"Oh, I'm so sorry," cried Laura. "I didn't mean it."

The two FBI agents helped me to my feet and offered to take me to the hospital; I refused.

"A few inches higher," said one of the men, shaking his head, "and you would have had a cracked skull."

I approached the older boy standing against the bedroom door. "I'm going to have to place you in a foster home temporarily."

"I know," he said, his eyes tearing up.

"It will only be for a little while," I reassured him.

"We've done this before," he admitted sadly.

With Laura alongside, the police officer and the Feds led the parade down the stairs—I followed with the two boys. Halfway across the street, the older boy broke away. He ran across the pavement and darted into a yard.

"Run, run!" bellowed Laura.

One of the men pursued him; the chase did not last long. They returned him to my car.

The Clark boys were no strangers to Mrs. Scott, a petite middle-aged black woman with a broad smile. Many times, due to Laura's erratic behavior, they had been placed there with her. She held out her arms to welcome the two boys and gave each a big hug.

The boys stayed in the yard playing with three other boys in a worn three-sided sandbox while I followed Mrs. Scott into the house. She told me that she had taken care of the boys on three other occasions. She also told me about Laura. "I can't believe how that woman could have such good boys," she said.

Before leaving, I had a talk with the older boy. He startled me by accusing the police officer who'd arrested his mother of killing his father. "She's gonna kill my mother too," he said.

It was after 8:00 P.M. when I finally returned home. I told Donna about the boys and how going from receiving home, to Laura, to foster homes, back to Laura and back to another receiving home would eventually ruin their lives.

"If we were to adopt," I said, "I would certainly consider those boys."

Two weeks later, I visited Laura at the Milwaukee County Jail. She apologized to me for whacking me with the phone and slipped me two tickets to the theater. Ignoring my section head's warning about accepting gifts from clients, I took the tickets, thanked her and was rewarded with her first smile.

Chapter 8

A Red Flag

Another pivotal year in my life was 1975. One evening, Donna and I attended a softball game at a local park. The manager, a fellow South Division High School alumnus, told me that he was one player short and pleaded with me to sign up as a ringer—I would be his brother Lance. Although I hadn't played for two years I agreed to substitute; I certainly wouldn't want his team to lose on a forfeit.

He put me at catcher, a position I had never played and never wanted to play. Fearing I would get hit by a foul tip or a bat, I knelt as far away from the plate as I could.

My first at bat came in the bottom of the second with two outs and the bases loaded; I lined a double to left, scoring two runs. I wasn't too concerned about the team's performance, a 14–10 loss, because after all I went three-for-four and drove in five runs.

The manager was so impressed with my performance that he pleaded with me to join the team as a regular.

"I'll play under one condition," I told him. "I want to pitch."

He agreed and after a two-year hiatus, I was back on the mound.

Despite my visual problems, I pitched well and batted .780, tops on the team. Defensively, however, was a different story. I never saw balls hit near me and seldom saw balls hit into the outfield. In fact, my vision had become so bad I couldn't even find the pitcher's mound—that's when the umpire usually ordered one of the infielders to escort me to the mound. My season ended painfully in the sixth inning of our last game when a well-placed line drive ended up between my legs.

That fall, I departed my old football team to play quarterback for another team. This time, it wasn't my eyes but my chronic left knee problem that prematurely ended my season and my football career.

That same year, Donna and I purchased our first house—a large old stucco duplex.

During my second week in his unit, my new supervisor assigned me to the Robins case. The neglect referral, classified as a failure to thrive, stated that a six-month-old was being neglected by her nineteen-year-old mother.

I met nurse Ellen Somers at the Robins house, located in a lower-working-class area. We introduced ourselves and told Alicia, the nineteen-year-old mother, about the neglect referral. She said nothing. She led us into the bedroom where her little daughter was napping in her crib. Unlike many of the other mothers, Alicia was cooperative—she voiced no objections to Ellen's examining her little girl.

"Are you feeding her enough?" Ellen asked.

"Yes, I think so."

"Are you following the instructions on the formula?"

"Yes."

Expressing concerns about the little girl's weight, Ellen insisted that we take her to a children's hospital. Since I hadn't seen the little girl before and since I wasn't a medical person, I decided to defer to Ellen.

Unlike other clients, Alicia did not object to our taking her daughter. In fact, she seemed to me to want her daughter placed at the children's hospital. "If you think we should take my daughter to the hospital, I'm for it."

While Ellen and Alicia talked, I phoned my supervisor. He referred me to our attorney, who then referred me to a doctor at the children's hospital.

"Don't pull the child," the doctor said. "I saw her the other day and she didn't look like she was losing weight."

My supervisor made it clear that if both the children's court attorney and the doctor were against the removal of the little girl, then I was not to remove her.

Ellen, however, disagreed. "If we don't take her to the children's hospital, she'll die."

It was quite a dilemma. Do I go against my supervisor, our attorney and the doctor or do I listen to the nurse? I thought a few moments—hell, I was going to take the little girl to the hospital where she could be checked. It was better to be cautious, especially when a child's life was at risk.

The next morning, my supervisor called me over to his desk for what I thought would be a chewing out or disciplinary action like a suspension. To my surprise, he congratulated me, telling me what a fine job I had done.

Apparently, the children's hospital had informed him that my removal of the child had saved her life.

"Great job, Phil," he said.

Knowing that I saved the little girl's life meant more to me than anything. Often, I think about some of the other children I took to be examined. I wonder what they're doing now and how they turned out.

I firmly believed that the mother did not intentionally starve her daughter. At the hearing, Alicia, a tenth-grade dropout, revealed that she could not read and was unable to follow the written instructions on the formula.

My tenure with my new supervisor was to be short-lived, thanks to another reorganization in the department. I got a new boss, another of those ex-Catholic priests who infiltrated social services.

"I noticed that you are a physical person," he said, referring to a photo on my desk of me flexing while posing in a swimsuit at Cedar Lake.

"I hope you don't go around beating up the clients," he said.

"No, just supervisors," I joked.

The Sklar case was the most bizarre I'd ever been involved in—an abuse case in reverse. Ben Sklar, a six-year-old boy, was alleged to have been abusing his mother, Wilma. Wilma, Ben and nine-year-old Dawn lived in a small first-floor apartment. At my first visit, Wilma, a thirtyish, pale woman who was an alleged alcoholic removed her blouse, exposing her bruised arms and shoulders.

"Ben beat me with a carpet sweeper," she said.

Apparently Wilma's drinking infuriated Ben to the point that he grabbed the nearest object—a broom, an ashtray, a carpet sweeper or whatever he could get his hands on—and beat his woozy mother.

With Wilma's approval, I had Ben evaluated by a child psychologist. He concluded that Ben was an extremely hyperactive child with an aggressive personality. One week later, I received his written evaluation: *Ben Sklar is a volcano ready to erupt at any time. Wilma's drinking triggers violent reactions in Ben, such as screaming and throwing objects. Her lying on the floor in a stupor exacerbates the situation. His reaction is to grab the nearest object, which he uses to strike his mother.*

Through the children's court, I was granted an Order of Supervision mandating that Wilma undergo alcohol treatment and that Ben and Dawn be placed in receiving homes until a hearing could be held. Wilma told me that there was no need to find a temporary home for the children because her boyfriend, whom the kids called Uncle Frank, would be glad to take care of the children in her absence. After some research, I found out that the uncle had allegedly molested Dawn and two other girls.

I placed Ben and Dawn in the Greenes' receiving home. The Greenes lived in a large house in a rural section of the county. The Greenes' six-acre lot with its animals—two ponies, two dogs and a cat—was what I would consider a child's fantasy. There was one problem; Ben and Dawn could only stay there for three weeks.

Reports on Wilma's medical status were not encouraging—it seemed that the children would need to be in placement for a long time. What I had to find was a foster home that could accommodate both children for the duration—the Gates home was recommended by one of the foster care workers.

The Gateses lived in a large house about fifteen miles southeast of Milwaukee. The Gates home was similar to that of the Greenes. Their large house was on a four-acre lot. Like the Greene home, the Gateses had several animals. There were two dogs, a cat and plenty of toys. The inside of the house was a shrine garnished with religious symbols and artifacts. Religious statues and prayer books were neatly stacked on small wooden tables. Crosses and holy pictures hung from the bedroom and living room walls.

Mrs. Gates made it a point to tell me how religious the family was.

"My husband Dan and I attend church three times a week," she said.

On a Friday afternoon I delivered Ben, Dawn and two boxes of clothes to the Gates home. Mrs. Gates and I took Ben and Dawn into the house and introduced them to a girl and boy sitting on the living room couch.

The following Monday I called Mrs. Gates to find out how the children were doing.

"Just perfect," she said.

On Thursday, I took Ben to a session with a psychiatrist.

"Being away from his mother is good for Ben," he said.

I was quite pleased with my handling of the Sklar case. Wilma was in seemingly endless alcohol rehab and Ben, undergoing therapy, was with his sister in the Gates home.

My self-adulation was short lived when my coworker informed me that the Gateses were being charged with child abuse. Dan Gates allegedly had molested two girls under the age of nine.

"Oh, it's true all right," said Mrs. Gates, responding to the allegations. "That's one of Dan's flaws. I told him, don't molest the children. But that's his only flaw. Dan's a good person—he goes to church. Besides, it's not like these are good children or anything. These are trash from trashy families."

The Gates home was shut down and Dan Gates was charged with child abuse. I began searching for another home for Ben and Dawn.

Later, I found that child abuse by foster parents was not unique to the Gateses.

It seemed to me a no-win situation. You take kids from one abusive situation and place them into another.

The longer I worked in child protection, the more disillusioned I became. It wasn't merely the clients or foster homes but the lawyers, the court system and especially the so-called behavior specialists like social workers and shrinks.

My declining vision made it difficult to do my job. Besides going into dark hallways, there was the problem of driving. Driving alone was enough of a problem but driving with children whom I had snatched was a disaster waiting to happen.

In August 1976, my coworker Jane and I removed three children from an apartment. While the abusive father was asleep, Jane and I, with the mother's help, snatched the children along with two boxes of clothing. Unfortunately, the father woke up before we were finished and we had to grab the boxes and the children and get away. Jane herded the children into the hallway. I picked up a large box of clothes and stumbled down a flight of narrow steps. We raced to my car where I tossed the boxes into the hatchback and Jane crammed the children into the back seat. We were anxious the irate father might be in pursuit—I didn't know if he was—but making my getaway I jumped two curbs and ran my car into a light pole.

In December of 1976, I reported to the Department of Motor Vehicles to renew my driver's license. A woman instructed me to look into a binocular-type gadget while she tested my peripheral vision.

"Tell me when you see it."

What was I supposed to see? I had already read the chart directly in front of me. She became testy—I said yes to whatever I was supposed to see and she passed me. But I didn't realize how serious not seeing that little dot was.

So I lacked peripheral vision—hell, I had never had good peripheral vision. I had always known about peripheral vision but I didn't think that it was important. After all, I played quarterback without peripheral vision and was still able to spot my receivers.

However, two months later everything came crashing down. My entire life changed forever on a sub-zero February evening in 1977.

Racquetball was the new "in" sport. Everyone was playing racquetball. Since I had played some handball in college, I accepted my coworker's invitation to join him on the racquetball court.

We started by softly hitting the ball off the front wall. No problem with that, so we went to the side walls—that's when it began. I missed every ball hit off the right and left walls, causing my coworker to remark on how uncoordinated I was. We tried playing a game. I was embarrassed and worried.

"I guess I need practice," I said, trying to dismiss my dismal performance. *Maybe it was my lack of depth perception*, I thought. Yes, that was it—my lazy eye was responsible for my not locating the ball.

Donna suggested that I go to an ophthalmologist whom she had seen several years earlier. I met with the doctor she recommended for the first time on February 16, 1977. He started by having me read the eye chart; *no problem there*, I thought. Then he brought out a small rectangular object with two lines in the center; that's when I began to worry.

"Which line is closer?" he asked. They both looked the same to me.

"Which one is closer?"

"The one on the left?"

He shook his head.

"No wait—the one on the right; no maybe the one on the..."

"You lack depth perception," he said softly.

"Depth perception? Maybe it's because of that lazy eye."

He shook his head, then told me he wanted to check my visual field. At that point, I began to worry that he was searching for something I really did not want to know about.

He instructed me to look into a large binocular-like object and tell him when I saw a small white dot against a black background. My neck and my stomach tightened, my forehead pounded and chills ran up and down my spine. I asked him questions to relieve my anxiety. He said nothing.

"Do you see it now?" he kept asking.

Straining, squinting and even scanning, I still couldn't locate that elusive white dot.

He pushed that binocular-like contraption to the side, then stepped directly in front of me; he wanted to make sure that I could see him.

"You have an eye disease," he said carefully, measuring his words.

"Eye disease?"

"You have an eye disease called retinitis pigmentosa," he continued.

Although I had never heard of *retinitis pigmentosa* (RP), I knew it had to be something hideous—something evil.

Then he went on with the clinical description: "Retinitis pigmentosa is a genetic eye disease." He paused, then continued. "The symptoms are night blindness, tunnel vision, lack of depth perception..." He trailed off and cleared his throat. "And eventually, total blindness."

Now wait a minute. Sure, I had some vision problems, was night blind, lacked depth perception and peripheral vision, but that couldn't mean I had some awful eye disease. Could it?

My visual field was narrowing, he said—how fast, he couldn't say. In order to find out, he suggested that I go to a clinic for testing. In my state of mind at that time, I didn't want to know anything more about my visual field closing. He also wanted a meeting with Donna and me to inform us about the possibility of transmitting RP to our children.

He went on and on explaining retinitis pigmentosa—I heard nothing. All I knew was that I had to get away from there. I sprung from the chair, shuffled out of that dreadful office and into the hallway and somehow managed to make it to the elevator before collapsing. That was the first of many panic attacks I suffered during that awful period.

A week later, Donna and I met with the doctor. He told us that we should seriously consider not having children. He believed RP to be a genetic disease and that we risked transmitting it to any children we might have. I countered by telling him that RP had never shown up in my family but he insisted that the risk of transmitting it to our children was great. He also told me that I should not be driving a car.

"He's a good driver," Donna replied, ignoring the four or five accidents I'd had previously. Donna also told him that she had seen no decline in my vision. She always stuck up for me.

Day after day, I checked my visual field. I usually stood in front of a mirror and placed my index fingers on either side of my head or took an object like a rubber ball or pencil and moved it back and forth—I couldn't tell if my visual field was narrowing or not. However, I became more aware of problems with glare, especially with the early morning and late afternoon sun.

In September of 1977, I was assigned the Cohen case. Sam Cohen, a parole violator, was alleged to have abused his wife, Kate, and three small children. In a phone conversation with complainant Paul Cox, the brother of Kate Cohen, I was told that Mr. Cohen had been arrested for assault and armed robbery.

"He's a real mean dude," Cox said. "He once shot me in the leg."

Mrs. Cohen wanted me to place her children with her sister and then she would file charges against her husband. I set up an appointment for the following Thursday morning at around 8:30 A.M. She assured me that it was safe since her husband would not be home.

At 7:30 A.M. the following Thursday, I called Mrs. Cohen to confirm the appointment. She sounded desperate; she wanted the children removed. She told me her husband was crazy and dangerous and that he carried a gun. Again, she assured me that her husband would not be home.

It was exactly 8:30 A.M. when I arrived at the Cohen house. I stopped briefly to survey the area, then I parked my car around the corner and returned to the house. Standing at their walkway, I thought of what Mrs. Cohen had said about her husband, about his violence. What was I doing there, with half an eyeball, going into situations that even the police avoided? I zoomed in on the porch; it had four wooden steps. The door was hidden by the shadow of the overhang. Slowly and full of apprehension, I approached the porch, stopped briefly at the bottom step and then proceeded forward. I stood in the shadow of the overhang, waiting for my eyes to adjust until I could see the door. *Here goes nothing*, I thought, rapping on the door, hoping she wouldn't answer—but she did.

Speaking softly in a high-pitched voice, she invited me into her home.

Ever so slowly, I stepped into a dark room and tried making small talk to give my eyes a chance to clear before moving. I turned to the sound of her voice and followed her footsteps into the kitchen.

"Please sit down," she said from my right. "There's a chair in front of you."

Nervously, I groped until I found the back of the chair and then slid it toward me.

She sat to my right and leaned toward me. She spoke slowly, measuring her words.

"I want you to take the children's clothes to my sister's house."

As she spoke, I scanned the kitchen and located a sliver of yellow glare coming from the backyard window. When my eyes finally cleared, I was able to spot a sink, stove and refrigerator.

Although she wanted the children with her sister, she voiced no objections to my suggesting the children be placed into a receiving home.

"As long as I can see my kids," she said.

Suddenly, I heard a loud thump coming from a door to my left.

"Oh no!" she shouted.

Squinting and straining, I barely saw the shadow of a large man coming straight at me.

"You ain't takin no kids!" he erupted.

Mrs. Cohen lunged from her chair and grabbed his shoulders.

"Run," she cried. "He's got a gun!"

I sprung from the chair and stumbled through the dining room, knocking over a table lamp and crashing into the doorway. I groped until I found the handle, then yanked open the door and leaped onto the porch, then down onto the sidewalk. Making like an Olympic sprinter, I darted toward my car, praying that I would not get shot.

Shaken, I returned to my office and recounted what had happened. The job was becoming more hazardous for me. Going into dangerous situations in dark areas was risky enough for a sighted person, but for me it could be treacherous. Had it not been for Mrs. Cohen, I might have been wounded, or worse, killed.

Chapter 9

The End of the Dream

Back in 1976 I had created several cartoon characters, including *Mr. Garbanzo*, a three to four-panel comic strip that featured one main character, Mr. Garbanzo, who was a seventh grade teacher in an inner city school. I displayed my comic portfolio to several Wisconsin newspapers as well as *The Chicago Tribune* and *The Grand Rapids Press*.

At that time, Milwaukee had two daily newspapers, the morning *Milwaukee Sentinel* and the evening *Milwaukee Journal*. In 1980, I received a call from the *Milwaukee Sentinel*'s editor. He had seen my work and asked if I would be interested in becoming a cartoonist for the newspaper. I thought about it and told him I would get back to him. This could be my big opportunity, my dream. I was euphoric.

Then, at an eye exam, the decision was made for me.

"You are slowly going blind," my doctor said. "They don't employ blind cartoonists."

The following week I called the editor and informed him that I wasn't interested in the job he'd offered. I gave no explanation.

Not only did vision loss prevent me from becoming a cartoonist, but it resulted in my having to make one of the most difficult decisions of my life. I decided to transfer out of Child Protective Services into a less hazardous area. The only openings were in Self Support. Unlike Child Protection, requiring me to bring children from Children's Court to a foster or receiving home, Self Support was a newly-created department where we were to place welfare recipients into job training, which they did not want.

The week after transferring into Self Support, I entered the hospital for my third knee operation. At the hospital I had an experience which further deepened my depression. Channel surfing the day after my surgery, I caught a glimpse of actor Ben Gazzara on *Good Morning America*. What caught my interest was that the actor was holding a black contraption that looked like a pair of large binoculars. Immediately, that red flag appeared—I broke into a sweat and began shaking.

"This is a device for people with the eye disease retinitis pigmentosa," he explained to host Joan Lunden.

I started breathing heavily—the room turned a fuzzy red; I was about to have another panic attack. *Oh my God*, I thought.

"Is there any cure for this disease?" the host asked.

"No, eventually everyone with retinitis pigmentosa, or RP, loses their vision."

"What does that device do?"

"In the initial stages of RP, the person afflicted has no night vision—this device will help them to see better in the dark."

Two weeks later, my attention was caught by another reference to the device. This time it was in a journal article. While waiting to see my orthopedic surgeon, I was leafing through an issue of *Psychology Today* when I saw an interesting graphic in an article. It had a peculiar red shading along the borders. Suddenly, my stomach began to knot up; there was that sinking feeling again. I read the print. It told of a pilot who, at the age of thirty-eight, experienced vision loss due to retinitis pigmentosa. By the age of forty-three, he had become totally blind.

As the days passed and my own vision problems increased, my moods worsened. Then while driving on the Menomonee River Parkway after a late afternoon home visit, I became so consumed with depression that I pulled over to the side of the road. I turned toward the river and listened to a train rumbling eastward. I felt that I was at the end. Everything seemed so hopeless. Why was this happening? How long would it be before I was completely engulfed by the dark? How could I support my family? What would I do? How could I endure? At that moment a voice came over the car radio; it was the national spokesman for the Council For The Blind.

"Persons with vision loss can be productive citizens," he said. "With understanding and the proper training they can do anything. They can perform any function anyone else can. If you are a visually impaired person, don't be discouraged—seek help; get the proper training. Remember, you can be a productive person." His words stayed with me.

One week after my knee surgery, I returned to work in my new area, Self Support, and was introduced to my new unit supervisor. He was highly intellectual, having been a math major, and he was quiet.

As time passed, I noticed a grayish silver haze on the edge of my visual field. My ophthalmologist told me that it was the RP and fitted me with a pair of dark green wraparound glasses, which he said would cut down on ultraviolet rays. The glasses were of no use to me. They were too dark to wear while driving and they were awkward. He mentioned nothing about the sparklers but he didn't have to. I know those sparklers were my visual field closing in. Those sparklers, along with bright flashes and dark floating blobs, now constituted my entire visual field.

At work, I took my coffee breaks in the cafeteria, usually sitting by myself, because I didn't want anyone around me. I didn't want anyone to know my dark secret.

At that time there were three blind individuals at my agency. Of the three, one was aided by her tan German Shepherd guide dog, while the other two relied on red-and-white canes.

At noon in the cafeteria, I'd study the three of them carrying trays of food to their tables and marveled at how they avoided bumping into obstacles.

Soon, I purchased my first pair of prescription sunglasses. After an eye examination, the optometrist told me I had old inoperable cataracts, probably from birth. He mentioned nothing about RP and I offered no information. The cataracts were responsible for the problems with glare, the night blindness and even the tunnel vision, I rationalized. As far as I was concerned, my days of worrying about RP and blindness were over.

One year later, I decided to purchase a pair of photo-gray sunglasses. I felt a better pair of sunglasses would help me navigate. But when the receptionist told me that I had to get my eyes examined, that cold chill resurfaced.

Entering the dark examination room, I bumped into a table and couldn't find the chair.

The optometrist had witnessed my ineptitude but said nothing. He shined a light into my eyes and had me look into what appeared to be a large pair of binoculars. I had no trouble reading the eye chart since I had memorized it before sitting down. I felt relieved until he pushed the device aside and leaned over toward me.

"We have some serious problems here," he said in a soft and grainy voice.

That dreadful feeling overcame me—I knew what was coming next.

"You have retinitis pigmentosa."

His voice, words and message pummeled me. The dark room flared into a bright red. My heart pounded and I became short of breath. I felt myself sliding from the chair onto the floor but did not bother to catch myself. He called the receptionist and they lifted me back onto the chair. Later that evening, Donna took me to a medical clinic where I was treated for a panic attack—my fourth in two years. The nightmare wasn't over; it only had been delayed temporarily.

One evening, I returned to my old neighborhood and walked the streets I had played on as a child. I asked myself, was I able to see better at fifteen than now? I walked past my old house and stopped in front of Slim's house, now occupied by another family. I drifted back to those summer evenings; sitting on the porch with my friends, sipping soda while listening to the Milwaukee Braves play-by-play broadcaster Earl Gillespie's voice booming across the radio: "And there's a long drive, back toward the wall, back, back, and it's a home run for Henry Aaron!" I wanted to dart up the steps and ring the doorbell as I'd done so many times in those wonderful days of my youth.

I trotted toward Burnham Street. Directly across the street was the old building that had once housed the bicycle shop. Slowly, I walked up the long alley toward my old house, scanning the houses and garages. Something was wrong— shadows appeared darker. Telephone poles, ash boxes and garages seemed distorted. Even the old red barn in the yard where my friend and I had tossed our ice balls looked different. It was like being in a bad dream—a nightmare from which I wanted so desperately to wake up.

The next afternoon, I drove to the park and walked to the boathouse that had once been my work area. The building looked the same: same worn yellow stucco, same old warped green door and even the same dead bugs stuck to the same dirty window. The gravel had finally been paved but the boathouse seemed unchanged. As I had done those previous summers, I entered the boat-house concession area where I used to buy sodas, ice cream sandwiches and popsicles. I seemed to remember the area, except for the three steps at the entrance; I stumbled and fell. My eyes had not adjusted. My fall couldn't have been because of my eyes. It had to be something else; I wasn't used to it—after all, it had been nine years since I had been there. *It's inconceivable that I'm losing my vision*, I thought. I was still in denial.

I didn't need any ophthalmologist or optometrist to test me. I would test myself. After all, I was the best judge of what was wrong with my vision—I would make my own diagnosis.

The first test was table tennis. After all, I had been the eleven-year-old table tennis champion at the Milwaukee Boy's Club and at UWM years later, I whipped everybody. I soon found out, however, that either my table tennis skills had diminished or it was something else. I had difficulty locating balls bouncing high off the table; the ball disappeared for a few seconds and when it reappeared, it was on the floor. It was the same with regular tennis; I had difficulty returning balls that had bounced high in the air or were hit to the right or left of me.

Despite the warnings from our doctor about our having children, Donna and I went about starting a family. Our first baby was a boy.

"Can he see?" I inquired of the nurse who was holding the newborn in a white blanket.

"They can all see," she responded, not aware of my motive for asking.

Next we had two daughters. All were tested for RP; all tested negative.

To me, losing my sight meant the end of my way of life. My appreciation of art, cowboys and sports heroes and, above all, my beloved comic books and their artists whom I wanted to emulate would be reduced to memories. It was all coming to an end.

There was the tunnel vision, lack of depth perception and, of course, the glare. I became a basket case whenever I had to drive during sunny days. In spite of all those problems, I wasn't about to give up driving—not me.

When my old car gave out, it should have been a warning for me to give up driving but it wasn't. Obviously, it was time for another car. Donna and I looked at several models, including a sports car, which she encouraged me to buy.

"Why not buy it, get something sporty?" she said.

It was snazzy and I would have liked to have it, but deep down, I knew I couldn't. There would be more fender benders, more collisions and more smash-ups.

Nevertheless, I purchased a new car. It was dusk when my father and I followed the dealer through the lot to the car. Moments before I reached it, I walked right into a cement pole; that alone should have been enough to prevent me from buying the car.

"Would you like to take it for a spin?" asked the dealer, handing me the keys.

"Oh no," I answered—I didn't want to total the car before buying it.

Indeed, if I couldn't drive at night, on foggy days, at twilight or on bright sunny days, then when could I drive? That question was painfully answered by the number of accidents I was involved in—eight in a three-year period.

The most traumatic occurred during a dense fog in May of 1982. It was about 7:45 A.M. as my car crept east. Vigilantly, I followed the taillights of the car in front of me. I drove like a ninety-year-old, riding my brakes until I came to a complete stop at the corner. Seconds after I accelerated, I heard a soft thump followed by a yell. My worst fears were realized; I had hit a pedestrian. Slowly, I pulled over to the nearest curb and got out of my car. I stopped and squinted. "Oh, damn!" I shouted, seeing a boy sprawled across the median strip.

"Is anything broken?" I asked, my voice trembling.

"Get away from him. Haven't you done enough?" shouted an angry woman.

Moments later a police car and an ambulance arrived. The officer was about thirty-five years old, tall and very friendly. He took me to my car and could see that I was shaken. He told me not to go look at the boy but he felt the boy wasn't badly hurt. I told him I was horrified and asked if he wanted to give me a breathalyzer test.

"Why," he replied, "are you drunk?"

"No. I just feel so bad."

The young officer smiled. "Don't worry about it; he'll be all right." He checked my driver's license, filled out some papers and dismissed me.

The boy's father, not as polite as the young officer, telephoned me that evening. Not mincing his words, he labeled me as a no-good son of a bitch who shouldn't be allowed to live, let alone drive. He told me his fifteen-year-old son was seriously injured because of me and that he was suing me for three million dollars. I tried to apologize to him but he kept going on about what a no-good piece of crap I was and he was going to make me pay for it. Nothing ever came of his threats, but that didn't matter to me.

Depression like I had never before experienced overwhelmed me. I swallowed what was left in a bottle of pain killers, chugged three large glasses of wine and went to bed, not knowing or caring if I would wake up the following morning.

Afterward, many of my evenings were spent sitting in a chair staring ahead, trying to measure my visual field. I laid in bed, dwelling on the next day's weather forecast. Would it be sunny, overcast, foggy or rainy? A sunny forecast kept me awake half the night thinking about taking an alternate route to work—I couldn't drive into the blinding sun. Fog was the worst. I was petrified of the fog.

One encounter with fog took place when Donna had flown to Grand Rapids, Michigan, to visit her parents. When I drove to the airport to pick her up, everything suddenly became dark and foggy. A man in the parking lot told me that all incoming flights were canceled. Feelings of terror strangled me. I sat staring into the gray nothingness. Here I was at the airport imprisoned by my enemy, fog, and I had to drive back home on the expressway.

Everything was dark. I had no idea where the ramp was or what I was going to do. Fortunately, I spotted a pair of taillights pulling away from the lot and followed them onto the expressway ramp. The further I drove, the more certain I was that I would not survive the ride home. Amazingly, I found my way home and discovered I had driven the entire way with my headlights off.

Day after day I dreaded driving to work. Just turning the corner of the street near my house was a major accomplishment—pulling into the parking lot across from my work building was cause for celebration; it was like the Green Bay Packers winning the Super Bowl or the Milwaukee Brewers winning the World Series. How long could I continue driving? How long could I keep up the charade of being a normal-sighted person? The future terrified me. How would I be able to live if I were to completely lose my sight? Not only would I have to give up driving but also drawing and reading and the unthinkable—my job.

It wasn't merely driving that was giving me problems. I was having trouble with my paperwork. The fine print on the new computer forms, particularly those in red and green print, were hard for me to see. I sometimes circled the wrong letter in the wrong field, which resulted in what were called "fatal" errors on the sheets. The M-25 block grant forms presented the most problems. Not only were those forms green, but we were required to fill out those forms in green ink.

Everything seemed to be coming apart: the auto accidents, the bumping into walls, doors and other objects and the problem with paperwork resulted in more panic attacks. I became paranoid—I feared that everyone was watching me, waiting for me to bump into a wall or a desk. It amazed me that no one seemed to suspect my sight loss.

Chapter 10

My Driving Obituary

My declining vision forced me to become a closet blind man. Word of my visual loss would certainly give management the excuse they needed to force me out.

Walking into doors and poles became more frequent, causing bumps and gashes on my forehead. Numerous auto mishaps resulted in an assortment of dents and scrapes on my car.

I concocted stories as to how my car became so fractured. A person slammed their car door into mine, causing the dents on the passenger side or the broken headlight; the scraped fender was caused by a deer in heat.

Despite the string of accidents, I refused to give up driving. But it wasn't merely the auto accidents I worried about.

After my mother's death, my father wanted to live on the east side of Milwaukee, which was known as Little Italy. On Sundays and holidays, we brought him to our house for dinner, which meant a day of watching baseball, football, basketball or any other sporting event on television.

On New Year's Day, 1985, Donna and I picked my father up for dinner and a day of bowl game watching. I plopped him in a chair in front of the TV while Donna cleaned out his hearing aid. He wanted to watch every bowl game he could, not missing a single play. While he sat fixated on the TV and Donna was cooking the turkey, I decided to take a walk on the Menomonee River Parkway near my house.

With the late afternoon sun to my back, I traipsed along the path, worn and icy from the hikers and cross country skiers. I continued up a slight incline, briefly stopping at the top to survey the area. To my left was the river, hidden in the cold shadows behind a dense thicket of bushes and weeds. To my right were trees, branches and bushes, extended from the powdery snowdrifts along the hillside. I was all alone. *Great*, I thought, *everyone's either drinking themselves into a stupor, watching the Rose Bowl or stuffing themselves; I've got the entire area to myself.* The "area to myself" words I would soon regret.

After about forty or fifty yards, I felt my feet becoming cold and wet. Suddenly, the hard icy path I was on became snow covered; the snow not only covered the top of my tennis shoes, but was well above my ankles. The more I walked, the deeper the snow. Somehow along the way I had managed to veer off the path. Wherever the path was, I didn't know. I scanned and scanned the white surface—I saw nothing; nothing to indicate that human beings had ever set foot in that area. No path, no ski marks, no footprints or indentations of any kind. Just because I didn't see anything resembling a trail or path didn't mean one wasn't there. With the bright glary snow added to my narrow visual field and lack of depth perception, I probably wouldn't have seen a divided highway, a freeway or even the Sears Tower, let alone a narrow hiking trail.

Wet shoes or not, I was determined to find that elusive path, so I continued trudging through snow-covered weeds and branches and over rocks. After another twenty or thirty yards, I stumbled into a cluster of trees. Many times I was told that being partially sighted could in some instances be more dangerous than being totally blind—until that day, however, I never realized just how dangerous. Grabbing the trunk of a thin tree with both hands, I stepped to my left to what I thought was a path—it wasn't.

Suddenly, I felt myself falling down...down... down. It seemed as if I was in slow motion. I fell about ten feet, bounced off a cement ledge, then continued my descent. I plunged into the icy river. And there I sat, wedged between two slimy boulders at the bottom, listening to the rushing water above me.

I was annoyed at myself for going out alone, especially in the late afternoon in the dead of winter. *Where the hell are your brains, Phil?* I asked myself. *You could be in a nice, warm house, sitting in front of the TV with your dad, sipping your third drink and watching the Rose Bowl.*

With hands on both rocks, I pushed myself upward. There I stood, my body numb and weighted down by my brand new leather jacket, a Christmas present from Donna, now covered with weeds and sludge. And before me, a herculean challenge—how to get out of this predicament. *You keep a clear head,* I told myself. *Don't panic. You'll get out of this all right,* I kept telling myself.

What were my options? Follow the wall east, toward the Wauwatosa village. That would be risky; the village was two or three miles away—I'd probably slip off the narrow ledge at the base of the wall and drown. I certainly couldn't go to my left—not into that river again. And even if I somehow managed to cross the river, there was another wall to contend with on the other side. There was only one way out; straight up, up over the wall and that was some thirty feet up. Squinting and straining my eyes, I saw nothing. Whatever vision I had before the fall was gone; everything appeared a dark, blurry gray.

Carefully stepping over and between the slippery rocks, I started back toward the wall. Several times I tripped, banging my knees and twisting my ankle, but somehow I made it to the wall, or what I thought was the wall. Reaching out and groping with my right hand, I tried to locate the wall—it wasn't there. *It's got to be here. Where the hell is it?* I took two or three steps, then slipped backwards, back toward the river. This time however, I didn't make the river—I slammed into a boulder. I was knocked unconscious. How long I was out I don't know, but when I awoke, I was lying on a large rock and staring up at the sky, which appeared to me to be darkening.

Pushing myself upward and leaning forward like a skier, I headed back to where I thought the wall was. After what seemed like an eternity, I stumbled into a hunk of concrete; the wall at last, I hoped. *Yep, this is it, the wall all right*, I assured myself, sliding my hand along the cold, hard, bumpy concrete. *Great, Phil, you found the wall— now what are you going to do?*

As I stood shivering, trying to get myself together, a dreadful thought entered my mind. Night was approaching and there was a real possibility that I might be spending the entire night at the bottom of that wall. I was in a bad way; along with my cuts and bruises, my Green Bay Packer stocking cap, gloves, tennis shoes, socks, slacks and jacket were wet and cold. If I didn't get out of there soon, I'd probably die of hypothermia.

I thought of those newscasts about missing persons, the ones who are found days after wandering away from home or from some facility, and imagined how my disappearance might be reported. "After six days of intensive searching by the police, the sheriff's department, the Wisconsin Air National Guard, the Wauwatosa Volunteer Fire Fighters and a Girl Scout troop, the frozen body of Philip DiMeo was found in a clump of bushes at the base of a retention wall near the Menomonee River in Wauwatosa, Wisconsin. According to his wife Donna, the forty-year-old DiMeo had wandered out of his Wauwatosa home on New Years Day. Authorities do not suspect foul play."

Donna—she's probably looking for me right now. Maybe there's someone on the path above me. There's got to be someone on that path, someone hiking or cross country skiing—that's it, a cross country skier.

"Help, help!" I shouted. "Is anyone out there? Help, help, help!"

I paused, cupped my hands, took a deep breath and yelled, "Help, help, help!" again.

I shouted several more times, then stopped to listen; no response, nothing but the faint echo of my voice followed by the gurgling river and the cold wind rustling through the trees. It became apparent that if I was to get out of there, I would have to do it myself.

Like the blind guy that I was, I groped and groped along the base of the wall, hoping and praying to God for help. "Please God, give me something to climb. A stairway would be nice, maybe a ladder or a rope; I'll even settle for a thirty-foot cable—anything. Well, what do you say?"

Then I remembered that the wall was old—it had been there maybe fifty years or more. There were cracks, bumps and crevices; maybe I'd reach an exposed cable or something.

I climbed onto the narrow ledge at the base and, facing the wall, started sliding myself to my left downriver. With each step, I rotated my left hand along the surface, hoping to find something—what I expected to find, I don't know. After about fifteen or twenty minutes and ready to give up, my left hand felt something. It was long and thin and it extended upward, possibly to the first ledge. From what I could make out, it was a blurry brownish yellow.

"A root, a freaking root," I shouted at the wall.

It made sense; directly above was a wooded area and the root had made its way through the decaying cement above, much like water from a leaky pipe will find its way through cracks in the plaster or through decaying shingles and rotted wood on a rooftop.

With both hands, I firmly grabbed it and gave it a tug—it seemed strong enough, but would it support my full weight and, more importantly, could it take me to the first ledge, twenty feet straight up? But what if it didn't go to the ledge, what then? What other choice did I have? I had to climb it—it was that or stay at the bottom, perhaps for the entire night or longer.

I thought about old prison movies, the ones with the inmates planning an escape. Like those prisoners, my only avenue to freedom was over the wall.

It was now or never. Reverting back to my rope-climbing days in the South Division High School gym, I grabbed the root firmly with both hands, ready for the climb. The adrenalin kicked in. For inspiration, I envisioned my old coach, in his blue and white Montana State T-shirt and gray sweatpants, at the base of the wall shouting encouragement.

"Come on, DiMeo, you can do it, come on, DiMeo—you'll make it."

Actually, I was the only one in my high school gym class who could climb the ropes without using my feet; I developed the technique of going hand over hand. That display of athleticism did not go unnoticed by the coach.

"Look at that DiMeo!" he'd shout, "He doesn't even use his legs."

Now, nothing could stop me; I was on my way up and hopefully over that wall. Everything was going well, that is until about halfway to the first ledge when the root snapped. Again, I fell backwards—back into that dirty, icy river. There I was again, sitting at the bottom with no hope of getting out.

Covered with mud, weeds, sludge and God knows what else, I raised myself and stood with water up to my chest, contemplating my fate.

After a few minutes, I waded through the cold rushing water, carefully sliding my feet over the slippery rocks hidden below. This time I had no trouble locating the wall; my chronically weak left knee slammed into the base of that hard concrete surface.

"God," I whispered, "Please, get me the hell out of here!"

Again, I stepped off the rocks onto the narrow ledge. With both palms and my nose pressed against the wall, I began my trek. Left foot left, right foot left. I continued downriver, directly below the heavily wooded area. After two or three shuffles I'd stop and, with my left hand, sweep back and forth, back and forth.

As I slowly shuffled my way, I noticed the sound of the river below had changed. What to me had sounded like a benign gargle was now a loud, menacing roar and growing louder. Adding to that were mini-waves of cold, brown water jetting over the tops of my tennis shoes. Very slowly, I lowered my left hand, then rotated my head to my left and glanced down.

I gasped. The only thing between me and the river was the narrow ledge. The rocks that lined the shore had been swallowed up by a torrent of brown. The further to the left I went, the deeper the river—one slip and I would be a goner. For a few moments I froze; not merely from the numbing cold, but from fear. For the first time I truly felt that I would not survive. At that moment, I knew that I was face to face with death. It was standing directly in front of me; cold, smelly, hard, clammy—blocking my only avenue of escape. It was behind me too; hissing, snarling, spitting and waiting.

Perhaps the law of averages had caught up with me. Notwithstanding the two emergency surgeries and the Chicago incident, those auto accidents alone should have killed or at least crippled me, yet I was reasonably healthy and in one piece. *Yep*, I thought, *the law of averages has finally caught up with me.*

Again, I weighed my options. Go back or continue. Go back—go back to what? If I continued downriver, there was a slim chance that a root from the heavily wooded area above had forced its way through the decaying wall and that root would be waiting for me—some chance.

After about ten minutes of shuffling down-river and groping around, I felt something brush against my cold left cheek.

A root, a beautiful root! My persistence had paid off.

Groping with my left hand, I felt another root, then another. As far as I could tell, there were at least three roots, all anchored somewhere above. It was here that I would make my stand—it was literally do or die.

With a new sense of confidence and determination, I grabbed the sturdiest root firmly and braced both feet against the wall. Like my comic book hero, Batman, pulling a rope from his utility belt, ready to scale one of those Gotham City skyscrapers, I began my ascent.

With each step, with each change of my grip, with each breath, I was certain I would not make it; I'd lose my grip, I'd slip or worse, the root would snap. Up, hand over hand, left foot up, right foot up, hand over hand, left foot, right foot I went, straining myself with each change of my grip.

Suddenly, I felt the root tightening. My first reaction was it was anchored somewhere below that first ledge—that meant the end of the line for me. Then, with my right hand tightly wrapped around the root, I reached upward with the left and, to my amazement, the root wasn't anchored below the ledge as I had feared, but somewhere above it. It took every ounce of strength I had, but

I managed to shimmy my wet, frozen body onto that ledge. The ledge wasn't solid as I had thought; in fact, it was littered with weeds, branches, broken glass, roots and bits of concrete—it was like sitting in the middle of a broken flower pot.

Though a bit wobbly-kneed, I managed to stand. I groped a little and found a cluster of roots from above. Again, I chose the one I thought was the strongest and started climbing. Hand over hand, my feet pressing against the worn concrete, I pulled myself up—up and over the wall. I was elated with myself; I had triumphed over nature. *I'm home free*, I thought, that is until I fell backwards over the other side. This time, it wasn't the river but the frozen ground that broke my fall and nearly broke my back. Stunned, frozen and half out of my mind, I reached down and felt the ground, hard as concrete—at least I wasn't in the river, but where the hell was I and how would I ever get out? Again, I groped around for something to climb—this time it wasn't a root, but an overhanging branch from a nearby tree. The climb was easier—I didn't have far to go.

"Hey, buddy," echoed a voice.

I'm hallucinating, it's not real, it's all part of the nightmare, I thought. Then I heard it again; telling me to stay still—not to move.

"Take it easy, bud," called a male voice. "You'll be all right."

At left, the grocery store that Phil DiMeo's father converted into a music shop, circa 1945. Phil's family lived in the rear of the building.

Above, Phil posed proudly after his First Holy Communion.

At left, Philip DiMeo and Donna Gilewski were married in 1973.

DEPT. ON AGING

Two of Phil's editorial illustrations

Phil's self portrait

At left, Phil and his
guide dog, Ladonna,
at their graduation
from training

Below, Kelly's Bleachers
were the 2014 MPS Co-Ed
Softball Champions.

Top row, from left: Mike Caron, Rachel Ploetz, Richard Hall, Steven Handrich.
Middle: Shawn Aston, LaSonya Maclin, David Bobke,
Phil DiMeo (coach), Tiffany Conway, Becky Redmond-Walker.
Bottom: Justin Groeschel, Ladonna (Assistant Coach), Jarod (Wood) Garner.

He reached down, grabbed my right arm and pulled me up. Though I couldn't make him or anything around me out, the brilliant circular beam from his flashlight reflecting against the shiny white surface caught my eye.

He introduced himself and said he was going to get me out of there. Firmly, he grabbed my right shoulder and steered me onto that elusive hiking path. As we walked, I caught glimpses of what appeared to be flashes of bright red that pierced the darkness. It didn't take me long to figure out what it was; the light from the roof of a squad car—I was quite familiar with that light. Since my night vision or the lack of it prevented me from seeing the car it was attached to, the light appeared to be something out of a sci-fi movie, spinning in mid air, spraying deadly crimson rays in every direction. It might have been just a light, but to me, in my pathetic condition, it was the beacon of my salvation.

My savior opened the door on the passenger side and slid me onto the seat, directly in front of the hot air blower.

"We'll get you warm in no time, bud," he said.

"You got quite a little lady," he said, referring to Donna. "She called us around 6:00."

"Yeah."

"Did too much celebrating, huh?" he asked.

"Huh?"

"You know; New Years celebration."

"I guess so," I mumbled.

At that point, I'd rather he figured me to be a bumbling, stumbling drunk than a bumbling, stumbling blind man.

"Well," he continued, "at least you had the good sense to stay off the roads."

"Yeah, good sense."

No sooner did we pull up to the house than we were greeted by a sobbing Donna.

"Oh my God!" she shrieked as I stepped out of the car.

Hell, I couldn't blame her—covered the way I was with all kinds of brown river sludge, yellow and brown weeds, twigs and manure all mulched together with a coating of snow, I must have looked like a cross between the Swamp Thing and the Abominable Snowman.

Donna and the officer each grabbed an arm, then steered me up the steps and into the foyer.

"You know," the officer said, "you should get checked out by a doctor."

"I'll be all right," I muttered.

He told me he'd give me a call the next day when I would be feeling better—Donna thanked him tearfully. He stepped to the door, turned and wished us a happy New Year.

I shuffled into the living room to where my father was sitting fixated on the football game with the TV blasting. I moved a bit closer, leaning over to where his good ear was.

"Dad, I fell into the river."

He said nothing. He just sat staring at the TV like I wasn't even there.

"I fell into the river, Dad."

Silence.

"I fell into—"

"I heard you!" he growled, still staring at the TV program.

"Swell." I limped out of the room and headed for the basement. Donna followed behind.

Together, we began peeling off the layers of my frozen clothes. It was quite an ordeal.

"Oh my God," she cried once I stood naked in front of the washing machine, "I'm going to take you to the hospital."

"What, and spoil our New Year's Day?"

She brought me a bathrobe, then led me upstairs to the bathroom. Using a warm wash-cloth, she gently patted my head, removing particles of dry blood from my scalp, then applied hydrogen peroxide and antibiotic to the wounds.

Donna still wanted to take me to the hospital. I refused.

"Why? I have no broken bones. Besides, what the hell can they do anyway? I'll be all right." But I wasn't all right. Although my entire body was battered and bruised, it was the emotional pain that consumed me. After Donna left, I swallowed the remains of a bottle of painkillers, chugged down four glasses of wine, then soaked myself in a tub of warm water for over two hours.

My string of mishaps did not end with that New Year's Day plunge; there were many more to come.

Thank God, I had finished my last visit and was on my way home. I had survived another afternoon behind the wheel without incident, or so I thought. Now if I could just make it home.

Like a ninety-year-old, I rode my brakes down what I thought was a narrow winding road of bumps and potholes. I crept along, stopping at every corner, intersection and driveway. I even stopped for shadows, fearful that they might be concealing a car or even worse, a person—I still hadn't gotten over hitting that young boy two years earlier.

Seconds after driving up a gravel incline and over a bump, I was startled by a loud metallic crash above my head. It took me only a few seconds to realize what had happened. I had driven through a railroad stop signal with the guardrail crashing onto my car.

The train whistle blurted out a warning. The ground quivered and my car died between the railroad ties with the crossing gate lying across the soft metal roof. At first, I sat stoically while the oncoming train rumbled toward me. I quickly regained my senses and turned the ignition key from off to on to off. Nothing happened. Depression set in; I thought of letting the train hit me. Why not let it all end on the railroad tracks? Self-preservation took over and I dismissed that idea.

The low-pitched whistle grew louder. It bellowed three more warnings. The ground trembled as the train roared closer, pounding the tracks. I twisted the key to the right. Thank God—the engine finally started. I revved it three times and tried to drive out but the wheels kept spinning, cutting into the soft gravel between the railroad ties. It took every ounce of strength I had to hold on to the steering wheel, violently shaking to the point that I was certain it was going to snap. I tried rocking the car by shifting from drive to reverse and back to drive—nothing happened.

The whistle blasted two more warnings and the tracks vibrated, rattling the car to the point that I thought the whole thing was going to come apart. *This must be what it feels like near the epicenter of an earthquake*, I thought. I shifted from drive to reverse to drive and finally rocked the car to safety.

In a period of less than three years, I was involved in eight automobile accidents and numerous non-auto misadventures. Another incident with glare occurred while driving to work on a bright, sunny August morning. While rounding a curve at about forty-five miles per hour, I plowed into a parked car whose driver was standing on the curb. I was unconscious for several minutes, wedged between the driver's seat and the dashboard. When I awoke, I felt blood oozing from my head and saw bits of glass scattered across the dashboard and the floor. Moments before the crash, the driver had stepped out of the car I hit; had he not, he might have been killed.

It was glare that caused me to drive into a light pole one Sunday morning. My forehead and cheek were bleeding. The front end of my car was crushed and so was I.

On a morning like any other, in February 1988, I started my car and began my trek to work. My usual paranoia over driving was present, but I felt an even greater trepidation than usual that day.

Slowly, I backed my car out of my driveway and somehow managed to overcome snippets of glare that temporarily blinded me as I turned onto Milwaukee Avenue—the first hurdle. The next hurdle: do not rear-end anyone before Wauwatosa Avenue.

Ever so slowly, I continued down Milwaukee, stopping at 68th Street—60th Street would be the next hurdle. If I could just get past 60th I'd be okay.

Squinting, I focused in on the traffic light; green with the walk sign blinking. "I'll make it if I hurry," I whispered. I took a deep breath and gently stepped on the gas pedal—so far, so good.

Then, the explosion.

"Mister, mister, can you hear me?" a young male voice asked.

I couldn't move. My head was throbbing and wet—I felt a hard wooden plank under me, my knees were bent.

I tried speaking. "I, I, uh, I."

"Yes," the young man responded.

"I, I, I..." I whispered before lapsing into unconsciousness.

When I awoke, I found myself in a bed at the hospital. My back and shoulders ached; my head, wrapped with bandages, throbbed and I had to use the bathroom in the worst way.

After my eyes fully cleared, I spotted the figure of a black woman standing at the foot of the bed; to her left was a young police officer.

"How are you feeling?" the nurse asked.

"I, I, I, have to pee."

"You know," interrupted the police officer, "you were not wearing your seatbelt."

"What?"

"You were not wearing your seatbelt."

"Huh?"

"You were not buckled up."

"I...I'm sure I had it on—it must have unbuckled after the crash."

"No, no it didn't—you did not buckle up. It's the law in Wisconsin, you have to buckle up."

"Yeah, yeah, yeah."

I looked toward the nurse standing beside him, shaking her head.

"You know," he went on, "I could ticket you, write you up for not buckling up."

Jesus Christ, I'm bruised, bloody, in pain, half dead, with my car totaled and this jackass is going to ticket me for not wearing a seatbelt.

"I'll give you a break, I'll let it go this time, but don't let it happen again. Now, about the accident," he continued.

Here it comes; another car crash to add to my list; another notch on my steering wheel, another lecture on road safety.

Then the officer said something that astounded me; it was the other driver's fault. According to the officer, two witnesses saw a large van run the light before colliding with my car. The accident wasn't my fault for a change. If I wasn't in so much agony, I would have jumped up and cheered.

When Donna arrived, I was still in the bed, sitting upright. The doctor recommended that I stay overnight for observation. I said no. I wasn't about to spend the night in that hospital. All I wanted at that point was to go home. All I wanted to do was to crawl into a hole. All I wanted to do was die.

"Can I get you anything?" Donna asked after we got home.

"No, I'm all right," I said, sitting in my recliner, staring at the TV. "You know, Donna," I paused. "You know I'm thinking that maybe..."

"What?"

"That maybe it's time to, to, to quit driving. What do you think?"

"It's up to you, Phil," she answered as she slowly walked over and bent down to stroke my face. "Just remember I love you."

Both Donna and I knew it was time for me to stop driving a car, but I asked myself, *What will I do now?*

Chapter 11

Learning to Become a Blind Man

G iving up driving did not put an end to my mishaps. It was dangerous just getting from one place to another. My forehead became a magnet for doors, walls, desks, chairs and even sinks.

The bumps and gashes on my head resembled those on my car before I gave up driving. I constantly had to come up with reasons for my bruises. I cut my forehead while shaving my eyebrows, I slipped on the ice and banged my head, one of the shelves in my garage fell on top of me or I was attacked by a group of irate Chicago Bears fans at a Packer game. The large gash on my cheek was naturally caused by a fallen icicle from an overhanging rain gutter.

To throw coworkers off the trail, I went out of my way to mask my visual deficiencies. I lied about noticing the colors of leaves or birds or even small flying insects. I made up tales about driving to Chicago or Grand Rapids or taking my car in for a tune-up.

One afternoon, a coworker whose car was perpetually in the shop for one thing or another approached me for a ride home.

"Oh I can't, I have to leave early to visit my pregnant wife in the hospital."

After that incident, I made it a point to avoid that coworker, especially in the late afternoon. I also avoided others, fearing that they wanted a ride or wanted me to accompany them on a home visit.

For the section meetings, I staked out the meeting room in advance to familiarize myself with the layout. Arriving a half hour before the meeting, I'd grab the chair nearest to the door to avoid bumping into anyone on my way out.

Even taking lunch or coffee breaks in the cafeteria became a problem. No matter how cautious, I'd bump into chairs, carts, tables and even people. Once, I drew the laughter of a young female financial aid worker after knocking over a large display at the entrance of the cafeteria. Whenever dealing with new employees, or employees from other agencies, I immediately extended my hand—I did not want to get caught off guard, talking while the other person had their hand out, waiting to shake hands.

At night, I sat in a chair trying to assess my visual field. It was like looking through a pair of binoculars with the black rounded borders or being in a small circular room with the walls closing in, like in one of those old matinee serials. The world was closing in on me and I couldn't do anything about it. It wasn't merely the walls closing in, but my whole world—the world of sight.

There would be no more sports, either as a participant or spectator, no more playing cards or chess, no more reading, no more watching TV or the old cowboy movies I loved and worst of all, no more drawing and painting. Life as I had lived it was rapidly coming to an end. Being a visual person, the loss of sight would be the cruelest of all punishments.

At work, I took every precaution to mask my vision loss. I was fearful that someone would discover my secret. No matter what I did and all the precautions I took, I felt my every movement was being observed. *You're just imagining things*, I told myself. Just relax, don't worry, no one suspects anything. That's what I thought, that is until March of 1989, when, at an in-service training session, a coworker made an off-the-cuff remark that startled me. The highly intelligent guy had been a county employee for many years, bouncing from department to department in search of that elusive promotion.

At that session, a middle-aged woman from a nurse's association told of her experiences providing services for the disabled.

"Working with the blind," she lectured, "can be extremely challenging."

"Phil would know all about that, wouldn't you, Phil?" my coworker chortled.

Now how the hell did he know? Was he watching me? Following me?

After that, I made it a point to avoid him whenever I could. But I kept asking myself—if he knew about my sight loss, how many of the other workers also knew? My every movement was being scrutinized, I feared. The more sight I lost, the more paranoid I became.

In August of 1990, we took our first camping trip to South Dakota. Donna drove, I sat on the passenger's side, the children and our dog Rusty were in the backseat. We camped in the Black Hills and drove into Wyoming. I wanted desperately to go to the Grand Tetons—both Donna and I realized it could be the last time I would ever see that mountain range or any other.

Unfortunately, our car broke down in Cody, Wyoming, and we were forced to return home.

My deception as a sighted person came crashing down in October of 1990, when the section head witnessed me barreling into a metal chair in a conference room.

During my eighteen years with Milwaukee County, I had occasionally run into this section head, mostly when I was in child protection, and when I did I felt uncomfortable around him. I don't know why, but perhaps it was his cynicism.

A week after the walking-into-the-chair incident, the section head arranged a meeting in my unit supervisor 's office.

"You seem to have problems with your vision," he said.

"I guess you could say that."

"I've heard that you frequently take the bus."

"That's no secret."

"I want to know what is wrong with your vision." He glowered and cleared his throat after each sentence. While he spoke, I could tell my supervisor was clearly uncomfortable with the situation, as he sat fidgeting with papers on his desk.

"I have trouble with going from a dark area to a bright area and I have some problems with depth perception."

He leaned over, stroked his chocolate milk mustache, cleared his throat and squinted. "What do you call this vision problem? Does it have a name?"

"Yes, it has a name."

"Well—what is it called?"

"Do you want the medical term?"

"Yes, yes."

"It's called...vision problems."

He insisted that I go to a medical doctor for an eye exam and that I provide him with the medical information. He assured me that anything I told him and everything in the so-called medical report would be confidential. Having been in the human services field for eighteen years, I knew one thing: nothing, absolutely nothing, is confidential.

One week after our meeting, I received a memo stating that the section head had observed me walking into a chair at a training session. It went on that he ordered me to see a medical doctor for an eye examination, the results of which would be given to him.

That flare-up and my refusal to submit a medical report resulted in my being denied a pay increment, one that was supposedly automatic. Later, for unrelated reasons, that section head was demoted.

The strain of masquerading as a sighted person was taking a heavy toll on me. I had trouble eating and sleeping and suffered a series of panic attacks. Finally, in January of 1991, I made another difficult decision as I had done when I quit driving: the decision to disclose my disability.

A secretary in the department scheduled an appointment with the new director. Needless to say, I was petrified about revealing a secret I had kept for fourteen years. How do you tell your employer that you want to continue working despite losing your eyesight? How did I know if I could trust her? After all, she could be just like the others in management.

On January 18 at 3:00 P.M., I met with the new director in her office.

"I have been a County employee for twenty years and I can no longer do my job," I began.

She tilted her head and leaned toward me.

"Why? What is the reason?" she asked softly.

"I have retinitis pigmentosa. I can no longer drive and have problems doing my paperwork."

She indicated that she was somewhat familiar with retinitis pigmentosa. She then asked me if I was computer literate.

"Not really, but I can type a little," I replied.

"You know, Phil, everything is going to be computers," she said.

If I agreed, she continued, she would send me for computer training at the special needs department at the Milwaukee Area Technical College.

She impressed me. I was grateful for any type of training I could get. But again, the question was, could I trust her?

Our department was rearranged again after that conversation. The new re-alignment meant a new supervisor. We were sent to the fourth floor cafeteria to meet our supervisors. It was all done by seniority.

When talking to my new supervisor, I blurted out, "I have an eye disease called retinitis pigmentosa. Do you know what that is?"

"What do you call it?"

"Retinitis pigmentosa."

He pulled a pen from his desk and began to scribble on his gray desk blotter.

"Never mind; the new director has all the information."

"What does this disease do?"

"It makes me blind."

Since there was nothing more to say, I sprung from my chair, stomped to the door, then turned toward him. He was fidgeting with his pen but told me he would pass on the information and be in touch with me.

I spent the next few months closing cases in preparation for a temporary telephone position in the newly created Information and Assistance Department (I & A). Seattle had initiated a pilot program allowing county residents to request services for the elderly by telephone. Using computers, social workers inputted that information, which was relayed to other agencies. The Milwaukee County Department On Aging wanted to copy the Seattle model and was in the process of creating a Milwaukee County I & A.

Our new director approved my pay increments and two weeks later hand-delivered the two retroactive paychecks to me.

On May 25, 1991, my doctor removed the second of two cataracts that had been with me since birth. Despite having a narrow visual field, my vision improved to the extent that for the first time in over thirty years, I could actually see colors. Taking advantage of the little sight I had left and using the acrylic paints the children had given me for Christmas, I painted several pictures of each of my children.

In April, I was referred to the Department of Vocational Rehabilitation (DVR) and assigned to a DVR counselor. She had worked with many disabled persons, but her specialty was the blind. We met twice, then she referred me to an optometrist who preferred the title "low vision specialist." He occupied a large office cluttered with all sorts of blind man gizmos. There were magnifiers of all shapes and sizes, mirrors, reflectors and clocks of all types: clocks with large numbers, clocks with magnifiers, Braille clocks, alarm clocks with buzzers, sirens, musical alarm clocks and clocks that crowed loudly like a rooster. There were spectacles with magnifiers and tinted lenses of all shapes and sizes. And rows of lamps.

He sat me down, had me read an eye chart and tested my peripheral vision.

"So you have retinitis pigmentosa," he said.

"That's what they tell me."

"Sure looks that way. Your visual field or what's left of it is extremely narrow."

I nodded and said softly, "I know."

"Well, don't worry," he said in a self-assured tone. "I've got just the device for you."

Reaching into a green box, he pulled out what appeared to be a large pair of spectacles with mirrors mounted onto a thick frame.

"This should do the trick. See the mirrors on the sides?" he asked.

I nodded. The mirrors he told me were to provide me with the peripheral vision that I lacked.

"Go ahead, try them out."

With both hands, I grabbed them by the thick stems and slid them onto the bridge of my nose.

"How do you like them?" he asked.

"They're kind of heavy. They're pressing on my nose."

"Oh, you'll get used to that."

"Yeah."

"Go ahead, test it out."

"Here we go," I said, raising myself up.

While I was stumbling around, the doctor kept maneuvering from side to side asking if I could see him. Hell, I couldn't see anything in front or to the sides. He kept shouting for me to use those mirrors mounted on the stems.

"Aren't they cool, just like side mirrors on a car. A real turn on with the chicks—wait till your buddies see you wearing those," he shouted.

"Uh yeah, I can't wait."

So fixated was I on the side mirrors, that I failed to see what was directly in front of me. After about five or six paces, I tripped over a stool, fell into a table and knocked over a lamp, a large mirror and an alarm clock. The lamp and mirror were smashed. The impact with the floor triggered the alarm clock. It happened to be the clock that crowed like a rooster. And it was deafening.

"Shut that thing off!" I shouted, sitting amid the broken glass on the floor.

"What?" the doctor shouted, "I can't hear you."

He darted over, grabbed the clock and started pressing the three buttons on the right.

He lightly tapped them a few times then tapped them harder. He eventually grabbed the clock by the back with his large right hand and then violently rammed the plastic face with the large numbers into the side of a metal desk.

"That did it; that took care of that sucker," he growled, glaring down triumphantly at the broken bits of plastic, metal and glass.

"Uh, I don't think these are for me," I said, removing the mirrored spectacles.

The doctor swept up the mess while I stood plucking the particles of glass and plastic from my jeans.

"Sorry about that," I said. "I didn't mean to break those things."

"Don't let it bother you," he chuckled. "It happens all the time. And besides, DVR reimburses me for these types of mishaps."

Before leaving, the doctor presented me with a small pocket magnifier with a light for reading menus in dark restaurants, a large magnifier for reading small print and a large heavy bar magnifier, more suitable as a club than a reading device. For my second and last visit the following week, I was given a pair of dark red sunglasses, a pair of brown wraparound sunglasses and a pair of yellow-tinted wire rims.

Chapter 12

More Lessons on Being a Blind Man

Centrally located on State Street in downtown Milwaukee, The Milwaukee Area Technical College (MATC) was primarily a trade school. It offered courses in welding, metal work, woodworking, auto mechanics and other manufacturing skills. It also offered courses in nursing and most liberal arts courses along with remedial courses in English and Math.

"Hey, can you direct me to the main MATC building?" I shouted after stepping off the bus.

"You're standing in front of it," hollered a young man.

That wasn't so hard, I thought, that is until I tried locating the main entrance. Back and forth, back and forth I went, but I couldn't find that entrance. Rather than asking someone, I continued my aimless walking, hoping to spot a group of students shuffling through some doorway.

"Hey you, sir," I said to a young man passing me, "Can you tell me where the main entrance is?"

"What's da matter, dude, are you blind or something?"

"Yeah, or something."

A young lady wearing a tan coat and a dark green hat witnessed my dilemma and quickly offered to assist me.

"Sir, sir, I'll take you there," she called, gently grabbing my right arm. She steered me around hordes of students, up some steps and through a large doorway.

"Here you go, sir," she said. "The stairway is to your right."

Room C-11 was on the second floor. I waited for my eyes to clear, then climbed the stairs. It shouldn't have been that difficult to find C-11, but it was. To me, locating a specific area had become very difficult, especially when I hadn't been there before.

I shuffled past rows of lockers and through students, stopping at every doorway, hoping to locate the elusive C-11. After turning the corner, I caught a fuzzy glimpse of several bodies shuffling through a doorway. Since there were no other rooms in sight, the room ahead had to be C-11. Making sure I didn't pass it, I slid my left hand along the wall and rows of lockers. *This has to be it*, I thought, stopping at the entrance of a wide doorway, bending, squinting and trying to read the room number.

"Hey, buddy!" a large man shouted from across the hall. "You're looking for C-11, am I right, huh?"

"Yes, I am."

"Follow me, buddy. I'll take you to C-11."

He led me down the hallway and into a large room. "Here you go, buddy, have a seat, the others will be along shortly."

He left the room while I sat alone at a large table, contemplating my future. What the hell did I get into? My participation in the special needs classes meant that I was no longer a normal person. Now, I was about to enter what was known as the blind network.

"Hey, man, are you a blind guy too?" a tall, pudgy young man with a red and white cane asked.

"Uh, not totally, but I'm getting there," I replied.

"Man, I'm totally blind; I can't see."

"Really?"

"Yeah, but that ain't bad. I'm able to make my way."

"That's good," I said.

I pulled out a yellow legal pad and black pen from my official Milwaukee County briefcase and began doodling. By the time I reached the bottom of the page, several others, all with canes, had come into the room.

After everyone was seated, the head of the special needs department addressed the class, then introduced the staff. There was the typing instructor, James, whom I had met in the hallway, my mobility instructor, Christy, and another who would be my Braille teacher. Jean was an impressive lady. Although I never cared for Braille or used it, I looked forward to those morning sessions with her and her Golden Retriever guide dog.

At our first session, she told me about how she had spent four weeks at the leader dog school in Rochester, Michigan. She and her dog had to go through rigorous training in order to be matched with each other.

"You would be perfect for a guide dog," she told me at our second meeting.

I attended the special needs classes four days a week. My lessons included one hour of mobility training, one hour of typing and one hour of Braille. This was the first phase in my metamorphosis of going from a sighted person to a blind person. Needless to say, I did not feel comfortable in that setting. Growing up, I fantasized about being a cowboy. I would be riding my horse that I had named Pancake—after all, all cowboy heroes had to have horses with names. Later, after my introduction to sports, mainly softball on the Alexander

Mitchell School playground, I would certainly be a baseball player. Still later, I would be a great quarterback. Still later, it was cartooning—I would be a famous cartoonist. Nothing could derail me from my dream of becoming a big-time cartoonist. Never could I have imagined that three-quarters of my life would be spent as a blind man—that I would even have to go to school to be taught to be a blind man. My gradual sight loss and introduction into blind society was, to me, my worst nightmare.

On the third day, my mobility instructor drove me to the Badger Home For The Blind to be fitted for a white cane. A man pulled from his pocket a tape measure and, like a tailor, measured me from head to foot.

"Yep," he muttered. "A 36 should do."

From what I could tell, everyone seemed depressed. The guy behind me tried to sound upbeat, but I sensed a sort of sadness in his voice. Maybe I was wrong—maybe it was my own negative feelings projected onto him.

"Here ya go, fella," said the man who'd measured me. "This is for you. Try it out." He handed me a folded red and white cane.

For a few moments I stared at it, wondering. Then, reluctantly I grabbed it and did my impression of a blind guy; tapping it on the hard tile floor.

Sensing that I wasn't too thrilled about the cane, Christy told me that the cane was my symbol of strength and independence. To me, however, it meant the exact opposite. It meant the loss of independence, the loss of strength and, more important, the loss of my pride. Displaying that red and white stick was like wearing a sign: Look at me, I'm a blind guy. That red and white stick reclassified me from a useful human being to another of those poor blind souls; the ones at Industries for the Blind, the ones whose entire day was spent performing such critical and challenging tasks as sweeping the floors, emptying the waste baskets, sorting out the pencils from the pens and placing screws into plastic bags.

"Using the cane will earn you the respect of others," Christy continued.

Respect? *Using that stick will elicit pity, not respect*, I thought.

"You know, Phil, every year you are entitled to a brand new free cane."

"What about the shades and the tin cup and pencils; are they free too?"

The man who'd measured me chuckled but my mobility instructor was not pleased with my remark.

"Now, Phil," Christy said, "you should be thankful that we're all trying to help you."

"Oh, I am. Just think, a brand new cane every year. That's one of the perks of being blind. I'm very fortunate. Unlike those poor corporate big shots, whose perks include a measly expense account, a private jet, a pricey wardrobe and free yearly company cars, I'm provided, at no cost to me, a brand new, state-of-the-art shiny red-and-white cane—you can't beat that."

At first, my mobility instructor worked me through the MATC hallways and up and down the stairs. Later, we worked the narrow aisles in the campus bookstore. Much to my displeasure, we worked the cafeteria where I had to navigate through groups of students and around tables, chairs and those large metal trays.

It was in the cafeteria that I was the most self-conscious—I felt I was on display, like everyone was watching me. I feared someone I knew was observing me—observing me groping around with that dreaded cane.

Oh, that poor blind man. Isn't that blind man Phil DiMeo?

Why yes it is. I used to go out with him. Look at him now. What a pathetic figure.

After a few days of tapping my way through the MATC campus, my instructor took me outside, where I was introduced to sidewalk and street mobility training. Christy had me stand on corners, listening to the flow of traffic to determine when the lights had changed. Even though I had limited sight, she wanted me to get used to using my hearing. The sound of the traffic was my cue to either cross the street or stay where I was. On and on she went, telling me that my white cane was a symbol of independence—all the motorists and pedestrians I walked past would respect me for using it. To me, however, the cane reinforced my negative feelings. It was a symbol of how far I had fallen and what a useless life I would be forced to endure as a blind man.

My time with my instructor always started the same; tapping and sliding the stick through hallways, up and down stairs, on elevators, through the cafeteria, the bookstore and along the streets around the campus. She also drove me to other areas of the city to familiarize me with different types of obstacles and situations I might encounter. Sensing my uneasiness with the mobility training, Christy took me to the Chocolate Factory and treated me to a bag of chocolate delights.

Although I was becoming experienced with the cane, I continued to be embarrassed. To me, it was a matter of pride—the pride of not wanting someone I knew observing me using that cane. Mobility training also resurrected an old fear of getting lost like when I was a young child. Somehow, I feared my instructor would leave me in some area by myself and I would become lost.

One afternoon, Christy wanted me to go upstairs to the cafeteria by myself and bring back an empty soda can. The prospect of stumbling into the cafeteria alone horrified me. At first, I told her I refused to go; she became angry. Sensing that she was about to start crying or worse, leave, I climbed the stairway to the second floor. Using the dragging technique she had taught me, I slid the cane across the hard floor and along the baseboard until I reached an open doorway. I tried to remember what she had taught me about using my other senses along with my cane. The sounds of dishes and smell of food was not too far in front, I concluded. Cautiously, I negotiated my way through the hallways. The sounds and smells were more noticeable. The doorway to the cafeteria was to my left. I was able to snag an empty soda can on one of the tables near the doorway.

When I returned with my prize, Christy told me that she had walked behind me and followed me into the cafeteria. That added to my feelings of paranoia that people were watching me.

The next day the head instructor called me into his office and said that he would assign me a new mobility instructor. He told me that my current mobility instructor thought that I did not respect her; that at first, I had refused to fetch that soda can. I assured him that I had nothing but respect for Christy—later I apologized to her and told her I was afraid of going to the cafeteria alone.

She apparently did not accept my apology. The head instructor replaced her with Jared. He took me to the Milwaukee Courthouse to meet a former student of his.

"Leave the cane in the van," he said. "You won't need it."

What was he trying to prove? He was up to something, but what? He made me follow him up and down the numerous cement steps outside the building. Behind him I traipsed; stumbling, tripping and scraping my shoes against the rough, coarse concrete. He was obviously trying to make a point that I needed the white cane.

We stopped at a magazine stand run by an elderly blind man. While I stood silent, Jared made small talk with him, bought a magazine and left for his van. Like a puppy dog, I followed behind.

After arriving back on campus, the head instructor sat me down and lectured me on dealing with my disability.

"He now has his own business," he said of the man who ran the magazine stand.

My own business? Selling magazines and newspapers? If this was his way of motivating or encouraging me to deal with my impending blindness, he was sadly mistaken. The man behind the counter reinforced all those negative stereotypes of the blind—all he needed was the dark shades and tin cup.

After that trip, I detested mobility training more than ever. *Once this instruction is over*, I concluded, *I won't use this damn cane.* And I didn't; the cane remained in my closet for two years.

My Braille instructor, Jean, had lost her sight at age sixteen. She was inspiring. Her independence and her resourcefulness were impressive. She had taught English in Indiana before coming to Wisconsin where she taught English, history and Braille. She frequently traveled on busses and trains and, wherever she went, her dog accompanied her.

Jean's quiet enthusiasm, sensitivity and tranquility impressed me. My Braille sessions were both inspiring and interesting. She brought books, tapes, records, Braille cards and movies as instruction tools. Not only was I impressed with Jean, but with the dog who, during those sessions, laid quietly on the floor; he displayed the same type of tranquility as his master.

Sometimes she and I just sat and talked. We talked about music, art and literature or shared our experiences as blind people. She was always upbeat. Having dealt with all kinds of people in the human services field, I could tell who was merely going through the motions and who cared. She really cared.

On Fridays, we gathered around a large table to discuss the various aspects of our sightless experiences. As hard as Jean tried to keep the group upbeat, those sessions for the most part were maudlin. Another student, Harriet, dominated the sessions talking about what a burden she was to her husband and grandchildren and how she was constantly bumping into objects and breaking dishes and glasses. Always so optimistic, my Braille instructor tried to put a positive spin on everything. She redirected the discussion when Harriet broke down and cried. Once, when I thought the session was becoming too morbid, I told the group that I was becoming so good at Braille that I could read the acne on my son's face and the bullet holes on inner city buildings.

On a more serious note, I informed the group of their rights under the Disabilities Act and that they could be quite productive in the workplace. We listened to tapes and movies and discussed their relevance to us as sightless individuals. Though invited, I avoided social functions like bowling or trips to a museum. Just being in Room C-11 was enough for me.

Within two weeks, I learned the first part of the Braille alphabet and improved my typing skills. My typing instructor, James, told me that one could not learn computers unless one had mastered the keyboard. Before MATC, I was a "hunt and peck" typist; after cane usage I referred to myself as a "hunt and tap."

My mornings started with me sitting in one of the open cubicles with my earphones snuggly wrapped around my head typing, while listening to my instructions on a tape recorder. At that time, my visual field was about one degree and I was able to read the screen but I was taught not to look at anything. After typing a particular lesson on the computer, I turned on the "deck talk" machine, which read back everything I typed.

The last week at MATC, one guy led by his German Shepherd took me into one of the attic rooms for a crash course in computers. As I sat in front of the large computer, the guy told me to switch on the screen and to put in a floppy. Since I had no computer experience, I didn't know where the hell the switch was or what a floppy was.

"What have you been doing for the last four weeks?" he barked.

"Learning how to type and that's all."

Then he showed me where the switch was and gave me a floppy disk to insert into the computer. However, he did not switch on the screen. His method of instructing was for me to learn by listening to the mechanical voice talk.

At MATC, I felt I had learned a lot and was anxious to put what I had learned to work; that is, except mobility training—I wanted no part of the white cane.

By that time I was relying on public transportation to and from work. On Mondays and Wednesdays, the bus stopped at Industries For The Blind. Eight or nine blind persons led by a loud middle-aged woman were directed onto the bus. Like a drill sergeant, she barked out commands.

"On the bus, get on the bus. Over there—an empty seat over there. Put your cane away! Do you want someone to trip over the cane?"

They all seemed so expressionless, so life-less, so morbid. Is this what I'm in for? Is this my future? I couldn't conceive of having a bleak future like that.

As I mentioned, most of them had menial jobs; packaging pens and pencils or wrapping shirts and sweaters. One lady in her late thirties boasted about her job on an assembly line. *How depressing*, I thought. *How could they get themselves up in the morning?*

What if I lost my county job? I would be forced to take one of those jobs—I'd be just like them—I'd rather be dead.

In March of 1991, I was transferred into the Information and Assistance Department (I & A). This was strictly a desk job—an "accommodate the blind guy" job—a far cry from my exciting days in child protection. In I & A my duties consisted of taking telephone referrals and inputting the information into a computer.

Early in 1993, our director—the lady who'd supported me and my disability—dropped a bomb. She announced that she would be leaving to join another agency. Sensing the morale in the department was sagging, one employee came up with the idea to create a newsletter, something to lift the spirits in the Department on Aging. I volunteered my services.

I thus became the cartoonist for the union newsletter. Although it was not big-time, like the position at the *Milwaukee Sentinel*, it was still cartooning. At first, my cartoons were one-panel editorial comments but eventually became eight to twelve-panel satires. Since everyone knew that I was blind, I titled my cartoons *INSIGHTS* and though they were sometimes met with controversy, they became a big hit.

The ultra-liberal union president ordered a telephone survey to determine how the union members viewed the cartoons. The results were unanimous—they all loved them. Workers stopped me in the hallways, called me and even came to my office to tell me how much they enjoyed my satire.

"As soon as I get the newsletter, I read your cartoons and then throw the rest of it away," said one worker.

An employee who suffered from depression said my cartoons did more for her than all her medications.

On April 9, 1993, while carrying a full cup of coffee, I walked into a secretary from another department. Although I didn't injure her, I spilled coffee on her dress. Two days later, the new director summoned me to her office and ordered me to use the dreaded white cane. She made it clear: either use a cane or find employment somewhere else.

Given the ultimatum of either using a cane or facing termination, I retrieved the cane I had put away two years earlier. The first day I used it, I caught some flak from several of my coworkers. Many seemed either surprised or shocked to learn that I was losing my vision. It took me about three months to accept using the cane while at work. However, I still resented the cane and never used it at home or when riding the bus.

In November of 1993, I received a call from a reporter at *The Milwaukee Journal* who told me that she had heard of the so-called blind cartoonist and wanted to do an article about me that would be featured in *Wisconsin Magazine*, a Sunday supplement of *The Milwaukee Journal*. It was around 7:00 P.M. on a warm Wednesday evening when she showed up at our house, accompanied by a photographer. She interviewed me for about two hours while the photographer took pictures of me sitting in a chair drawing or trying to draw.

The three-page article, which was titled "Declining Vision Hasn't Stopped Cartoonist," appeared in the December 3 issue of *Wisconsin Magazine*.

By January of 1995, my job duties consisted of guardianship, monthly phone contacts and checking the obituaries in the newspaper with our computer files. I did the best job I could—it was certainly better than sweeping floors, emptying garbage or working on an assembly line.

In April of 1996, our director announced that she was leaving. On June 28, 1996, a party was given in her honor and on the following day she departed the Department on Aging forever. I sent her one of my hand-drawn cartoons with a color picture of her and the caption: *You Will Be Missed.*

My remaining eyesight, however, was worsening. In order to continue drawing, I had to rely on special lamps, magnifiers and ultra-dark markers. Unable to see the tip of my drawing pen any longer, I eventually resigned as the union cartoonist. My last cartoon, a parody of *The Night Before Christmas*, would appear in the December 2003 issue of the Local 645 newsletter.

Chapter 13

Coaching Co-Ed Softball by the Braille Method

On March 16, 1994, I attended the first softball team meeting in Room 110 of the old Schlitz building, the home base of our agency. One of the workers had come up with the idea of forming a departmental co-ed softball team and would be the manager.

At that meeting there were three males with softball experience and two females who had never played softball. The manager would handle the money, the sign-up cards and the schedules. What he needed, however, was someone to coach the team, someone to recruit players, someone to conduct practices and above all, someone to deal with the bitching of players—duties no one was interested in.

I told the manager I had coached boys, girls and men's softball and won championships at all levels, but I had never thought of sports where women and men were co-participants. Although I hadn't coached a team of any kind for years, I was confident that I could do a respectable job. At that first meeting, the manager guaranteed us that he would recruit an entire team by the end of the week.

Donna and I talked it over. She felt that I should get back into sports, even if I couldn't participate. Three days after the meeting, I agreed to be the coach. I made it clear that I wouldn't be able to be a part of sign-up cards or collecting money; I would just be coaching the team. I was getting closer to actually accepting my vision problems and moving ahead with my life.

We took the last spot in the MPS Co-ed Softball League. The team had everything: a sponsor, a manager, a coach, caps and purple jerseys with the team name. The only thing it lacked was players—the manager assured me that he would take care of that; he frantically searched the building for bodies, most of whom were women. He combed the first floor, going from office to office with sign-up cards. His goal was to sign up as many young, attractive ladies as he could. Whether they could play softball didn't concern him, he just wanted women—as many as he could get; at that time, the league allowed a maximum of twenty-one players per roster.

I scheduled three Saturday morning practices for the three weeks before the season opened in the last week of April. I was extremely nervous before the first practice in that I didn't know how, without sight, I would be able to evaluate the players.

A coworker drove me to the field, the same field on which I had practiced both baseball and football for many years. While circling the park, I squinted and searched my memory, but was unable to recognize any area of the field. That was the field where I had practically grown up playing and nothing was familiar. I knew that all the landmarks were there but, because of my diminished vision, I felt I was in a foreign land or on another planet.

He led me to the bench behind the backstop where about five of the prospective players were warming up. More players arrived, identified themselves to me and darted onto the infield. While sitting, listening to the chatter of those so-called players warming up, I became more comfortable with my surroundings and concentrated on what I wanted the players to do.

My thoughts drifted away from my visual problems to what problems I might have with this team. Four players were over the age of fifty and seven were over forty-five. In addition, many players had not touched a ball or bat for years. I was pleasantly surprised when a young lady grabbed my arm and introduced herself to me. Her voice was perky. She said she was an infielder, but would play anywhere I wanted her to. She even offered to run bases during an infield drill. She went to the mound to pitch batting practice.

"I'll do anything you want me to," she said.

Out of that crew there were three guys who I considered to be pretty good ballplayers. A twenty-eight-year-old social worker in youth services was a decent fielder and a good contact hitter. He was able to play both shortstop and the outfield. The manager was a good contact hitter and an average fielder. He promoted himself as this super ballplayer and demanded that he play shortstop. A forty-five-year-old coworker had played softball for many years. He was a line-drive-up-the-middle hitter. He could play any infield position and, if necessary, could pitch. He became our pitcher after the second game in 1994 and finally retired after sustaining a torn rotator cuff in 1997.

Two women were good players; the other females were inexperienced. But the best was Celia, the woman who was willing to play anywhere. She was a left-handed batter who had mastered the swinging bunt that she artfully laid down between home and third. Since she batted from the left side, her speed allowed her to reach first base before her slow rollers could be retrieved.

At that time I really didn't know what I was doing or what the team was all about. Were we to go out and have fun or were we to go out and try to win games? At 6:00 P.M. the following Wednesday, The Milwaukee County Department on Aging took the field against our first opponent. I rode with the manager.

He led me to the bench where I tried to put together some type of line-up. Every five seconds, I asked who was there and who was still up in the parking lot, a ritual that continues to this day.

At game time, I managed to field a team of five women and five men. "We're here to have fun. I don't want anyone getting hurt—don't slide," I warned.

Despite the other team's power and our ineptness, we went into the last inning trailing only 10–7. In that final inning, our fatigued pitcher kept walking their batters. With the bases loaded, one of the behemoths launched a ball into the next county—we lost 14–7.

We also lost the next two games and some of the players wanted me replaced. But I wasn't about to step down.

"I guarantee we'll win our next game," I told the manager.

In order to increase the team's chances for success, I needed more experienced ballplayers.

I benched all the inexperienced players, brought in ringers and managed to salvage the season by winning ten of our last eleven games for a 10–4 record, which put us in a second-place tie. On August 1, the league scheduled a playoff. Although we were playing for second place, everyone was excited. Several of the Department on Aging big-shots attended the event.

We defeated our opponent 16–7 and finished the season 11–4, good for second-place trophies. On September 28, 1994, I held my first of many team parties. Along with the trophies, I presented the players with gag gifts.

"Next season," I promised, "we will win the championship." I was true to my word: in 1995 we finished 13–1 and won our first title.

In November 1995, while on my way to the coffee pot, I heard what sounded like a muffled explosion coming from one of the offices along the wall. Suddenly, I felt the hands of someone grabbing my shoulders and pushing me into one of the cubicles.

"My room is flooded!" shouted my usually mild-mannered coworker.

Then there was another explosion. Water was shooting out of the wall and flowing into the aisle where I was standing. Within seconds, I felt warm water streaming across my shoe tops.

Dragging my cane along the back wall, I managed to reach the office of my supervisor. At first, he did not believe what I had told him until the third explosion. Then he bolted from his chair when the fourth explosion occurred. Hot water from above gushed onto his computer, flowed across his desk and onto the floor.

It was unbelievable: walls were exploding; hot water was flowing everywhere. Ceilings hissed and crackled as water shorted the wires. One of the ladies sat trapped in her office while a torrent of scalding water from above blocked the doorway. She did, however, manage to escape under a large umbrella provided by one of the secretaries.

Sliding my cane from side to side while I sloshed through the flooded cubicles, I tried to get back to my office. The supervisor, shouting from somewhere behind me, warned me of live wires on the floor.

All hell broke loose. People sloshed through the water pulling files and covering computers with garbage bags or anything they could find. Strangely, the calamitous flood spared my office.

Supervisors waded through cubicles picking up folders, case records—trying to salvage files. Ignoring warnings from sheriff's deputies, one returned to his office to retrieve his computer. Complying with the sheriff's order, we evacuated the first floor and were out of the building by 11:00 A.M.

When I returned the following morning, I found the first floor in shambles. Personnel were retrieving soggy files and case records, pushing metal carts over the plastic tarp on the floor. In their offices, the supervisors were using vacuum cleaners to dry their desks and floors. Out of all the offices in my area, mine was the only one that was not touched.

The entire 1996 softball season was a disaster. When it mercifully ended, we finished in third place with a 9–5 record, my worst in twenty years. After much deliberation, I decided to coach the team for one more season. If I were to win another championship, I would have to get better players.

The co-ed team got a new sponsor. Unfortunately, a new sponsor was not enough to avert another poor season. In 1997, our first season as Kelly's Bleachers, we ended up with ten wins against four losses and another second-place finish.

In March of 1998, I was transferred to an area on the third floor. Every morning, I rode the small freight elevator to my third floor work area. One of the secretaries often asked me how much I could see. At first I was polite in my responses. "Not much" or "Very little," I'd say.

One morning she followed me onto the elevator.

"How do you know which floor to get off at?" she asked.

"By counting," I replied. "For example, I count to twenty. If the elevator stops at fourteen, than I'm on the second floor, if the elevator stops at twenty, I'm on three."

"What if that doesn't work?"

"Then by listening. If the elevator begins vibrating, I'm on the second floor; when the vibrating turns into rattling, I'm on the third."

"What if that doesn't work?"

"Well, if counting and listening doesn't work, I simply look at the numbers."

In 1998, I took drastic steps to improve the team. I drew a cartoon with four ladies in Kelly's uniforms standing on a baseball field. In bold letters above the picture was: I'M LOOKING FOR A FEW GOOD WOMEN. Below that I printed my work and home phone numbers.

Donna taped five of these posters on walls at the bar—two were taped up in the ladies' room and it was from one of those that I recruited two of my starting outfielders.

The team finished with an 11–3 record, tying us for second place. The league scheduled a playoff on August 12—we responded with a 19–4 rout.

We won the league championship for the next three years. I was interviewed by WTMJ-TV news anchor Bill Taylor for his *Positively Milwaukee* televsion show.

My 2002 team won the championship title again with a perfect 14–0 record. Several teams

complained that we were too good for our league—
most of our players agreed. After winning our
fourth straight championship and going unde-
feated for the third straight year, it was time to
enter a more competitive league even if it meant
jeopardizing our winning streak, which stood at
forty-six.

Even though I was successful as a softball coach, I
could no longer ignore the sad reality: I was going
blind.

My thoughts often returned to how early in
my life I had experienced an inkling of what was
now coming to pass. At age four or five, it was evident that I had the beginnings of vision problems.
At first, it was poor light-to-dark adaptation.
Whenever entering a dark building like a church
or a movie theater, I had to be led by my parents,
my older sister or one of my buddies. It was also
evident at an early age that I had a narrow visual
field. Whenever walking, I had to stand behind
my mother or sister or hold their hands; I could
not locate objects to the right or left of me.

I remembered how the specialist diagnosed
me with having a lazy left eye, an inherited trait
from my paternal grandmother. A pair of wire
rims would ultimately correct my vision problems, we were told. Although I had little difficulty
reading small print or dates on the coins I col-
lected when I was young, I couldn't locate fly balls

at the Milwaukee Braves games my father took me to or as an outfielder on a hardball team.

The memories wouldn't leave my mind. I looked back now at how, after a week of tests at age fifteen, another specialist confirmed the lazy eye diagnosis and even went so far as to predict my eyes would improve as I got older. It was at age twenty-four that I discovered I had tunnel vision.

"A pair of contact lenses will take care of that problem," promised the specialist.

Then, at age thirty-two, I was first diagnosed by the ophthalmologist I consulted as having classical RP. Retinitis pigmentosa (RP) is a degenerative, inherited eye disease that leads to severe vision impairment and typically results in blindness. The progress of RP can vary. Some individuals exhibit symptoms as infants while others may not show the effects until later in life. The later the onset of RP, the more rapid the deterioration can be. RP has no known cure.

Those who do not have RP have approximately 100 degree peripheral vision; some with RP have significantly less than 90 degrees.

A form of retinal dystrophy, RP is caused by abnormalities of the photoreceptors (rods and cones) or the retinal pigment epithelium (RPE) of the retina. Affected individuals may experience poor light-to-dark or dark-to-light adaptation and nyctalopia (night blindness). The deterioration of the visual field is referred to as "tunnel vision."

Sometimes, central vision is lost first, causing the individual to look at objects sidelong.

I had all the classical symptoms—night blindness, tunnel vision, poor light-to-dark adaptation, colorblindness and a lack of depth perception. Two years later, I was found to have cataracts, which had not been earlier diagnosed.

At thirty-four, two years after the original diagnosis of RP, I was experiencing difficulty with glare and noticed a brownish haze on the edges of my vision. Another ophthalmologist confirmed the RP diagnosis and provided me with a pair of dark green wraparound sunglasses; this was to protect me from harmful ultraviolet rays and possibly slow down the progression of RP.

As I approached forty, the haze I'd suffered earlier began changing; not only were the edges rounded, but the color went from a dull brown to a sparkling gray—that hideous sparkling mass was advancing toward the center and there was no known treatment that could stop it.

Later, when I was in my fifties, the deterioration of my sight accelerated. I went from barely seeing slivers of light from lamps and car headlights to total blindness.

At present it is not darkness but sparklers—gray and black heart-shaped blotches along with bright flashes followed by dark streaks—that I see. Within seconds, a bright patch I am looking at dissolves into a dark blob; then the blob changes shape and dissolves into what appears to be a dark grey cloud. A flash of light or a jagged black streak follows. Whether my eyes are open or closed, I cannot escape from the bombardment of those grotesque images. Many times I have looked toward a wall thinking I was seeing the sunlight reflecting off the window and many times I have crashed into a wall walking toward what I thought was light from an open doorway of another room.

After an extensive examination, a renowned retina specialist told me that I was hallucinating, but not in the usual sense of the term. What I was experiencing was the result of my retinas shutting down. My symptoms are not unusual for people experiencing sight loss, particularly those individuals over sixty. Although there is currently no cure for RP, there is ongoing research in treatment methods, some of which include computer chip implants, stem cell injections and vitamin therapy.

Chapter 14

Going to the Dogs

One of the secretaries at the agency, Janine, had a tan German Shepherd guide dog. Like clockwork, she'd enter the cafeteria at 11:30 A.M., with Pudding, her dog, directly to her left and proceed to place dishes of food onto a large plastic tray, which she would then slide to the cashier at the front of the line. I would stare in amazement at how Pudding, calmly at her side, led her around chairs, tables, carts of dishes and especially people.

I admired her, particularly her independence, not only with the dog, but her non-reliance on others. Sure, while she had one of her friends carry the tray of food to one of the tables, she did most everything else by herself.

Now, like Janine, I was blind. Like Janine, getting a guide dog became something frequently on my mind.

Several years before, our department had moved out of the old welfare building. Our offices were now in the Schlitz Building on King Drive. A year after my transfer, Janine had also been transferred to the Schlitz building. Not only did she become a secretary in our department, but her workstation was directly in front of mine—the only thing separating us was a metal partition that served to demarcate the many cubicles.

With Pudding at her side, she usually arrived at around 8:00 A.M. While she worked, she kept Pudding tethered to the desk. I was impressed with how Pudding behaved all through the day; he never groaned, snorted or most importantly, had an accident. Pudding's reprieve from lying next to the desk was at lunch time, when she guided Janine to the fourth floor cafeteria and then to the smoking room.

Janine later became bored or dissatisfied with her job and quit. I was given her computer and deck talk machine in compliance with the Americans With Disabilities Act.

In 2003, I met up with Janine and her guide dog in the backseat of a taxi cab. Among the things we talked about was me getting a guide dog. She told me of the schools in Michigan, Ohio, New Jersey, Oregon and California. I chose Guide Dogs for the Blind in San Rafael, California.

The liaison told me she would send me a three-page form requesting a physical exam, a tuberculosis test, an ophthalmologist report, a report verifying that I had passed a mobility course and names and addresses of three persons as witnesses to my blindness.

To assess my mobility skills with the dreaded white cane, I was required to walk eight or nine blocks. The route had to include at least one intersection with a traffic light. For my destination, I chose a small restaurant. The route included walking across 83rd Street, around the corner on Kenyan Street and down Ludington Avenue to North Avenue.

I began my trek. "I can do this with my eyes closed," I murmured to my daughter, who had come with me.

All I had to do was stay in the middle of the sidewalk. That would be accomplished by sliding my cane from the grassy lawn to the grassy curb. That worked all right, until I came to a cement driveway and wandered into the street. My daughter steered me back to the sidewalk and we continued. It was an easy straight shot until I wandered into someone's yard.

We made it to North Avenue and then crossed Ludington Avenue, where I veered into a parking lot. It took a while but we managed to reach the sandwich shop. After supper and on weekends, I practiced the route with Donna and my two girls and felt confident that I could pass the mobility test. On June 22nd, they called to tell me I would be interviewed at my home sometime in July and, after the interview, would be evaluated on my mobility skills. It wasn't meant to be a test but an assessment of how well I was able to use a cane, she said. I thought of the other blind man who worked in the Schlitz building, wildly swinging his cane into walls, doorways, windows and anyone in front or to the side of him. On July 25, 2004, I met with the instructor.

"This is just an assessment, not a test," he reassured me.

He gave me an overview of the guide dog program. He explained what was expected of a guide dog and how a guide dog could benefit me.

After a stop at the restroom and a "Good luck" from Donna, we started out for the sandwich shop. With the instructor trailing behind, I managed to make it across 83rd Street and onto Ludington. Everything was going smooth until halfway between 85th and 86th Street, when some idiot pushing an electric lawnmower ran into me. Trying to sidestep him, I veered onto Ludington and was nearly hit by a bus. The instructor steered me back to the sidewalk and we continued. Sensing my frustration, he told me to continue and assured me that I was doing fine.

Along with my inability to locate sloping curbs, I occasionally veered into someone's yard or driveway.

"A guide dog will do you good," he said. "You have problems walking a straight line."

We crossed Ludington, walked a half block and then stopped.

"You can put that cane away," the instructor said.

Then he handed me a leather leash and had me clip it to a harness he had brought along.

A few words about this particular type of harness: manufactured in Switzerland, the basic harness is mostly composed of leather with some plastic and metal. There are three parts. The body is a large leather loop used to secure the dog's head, neck and back. It comes in five different sizes. Then there's the belly strap. When the body of the harness is resting securely on the dog's back, the leather belly strap, attached on the left side of the loop, is slipped under the dog's belly and fastened to a plastic clip. Like the body, there are five different lengths for the belly strap. The strap is adjustable and can be a good indicator of whether the dog is either gaining or losing weight. Lastly, the leather handle comes in various lengths and can be removed without taking the entire harness off. This allows the dog to fit into cramped areas on planes, trains and cars. There are three types of handles: standard, offset and ergonomic. On the standard handle, the bars and leather grip are straight. The offset, with bars extending slightly to the right, keeps the handler over to the right, thus avoiding bumping the dog or stepping on the right rear paw. The ergonomic handle is slightly bent, which allows it to conform to the natural contour of the hand.

Next my instructor went over the obedience and guide commands. The obedience commands—"Heel," "Sit" and "Down"—are used when the dog is leashed but not in harness. The guide commands, used when the dog is working in harness, are "Forward," "Halt," "Left" and "Right." The command "Hop up" is used to get the dog's attention when it loses focus while working.

The first of the obedience commands, "Heel," is used to position the dog to the handler's left. With the leash in the left hand and the dog in the heel position, the handler may command "Sit," or "Down," where the dog lowers its body to the ground. "Up" returns the dog back to the standing position.

Then there are the guide commands. With the harness handle in the left hand and the strap between the first two fingers, the handler commands "Forward" to get the dog moving. If at any time the handler wishes to stop, the command "Halt" is used. If the handler feels the dog is distracted, the command "Hop up" is used to re-focus the dog. If the dog does not respond, the handler halts the dog, tightly grabs the strap with both hands and pulls slightly to the left; this is called the "time out." After ten seconds, the handler grabs the harness handle and commands the dog forward.

Body position is extremely important when working with a guide dog. If the shoulders, hips, or feet are not properly positioned, the dog may lead the handler astray.

To make a sharp right turn, the handler drops back the left or lead foot, rotates to the right and commands "Right." For left turns, the handler again drops back the left foot, but this time rotates to the left and commands "Left." When the handler wants the dog to take him to a specific object like a doorway, the handler slows down, turns slightly in the direction he wants to go and commands "Right, right, right" or "Left, left, left."

When working at intersections, the handler needs to employ the three P's: PAUSE, PROBE and PRAISE. When stopped at an intersection, pause to make sure the dog took you to where you want to be. Then, with the left foot, probe to make sure you are at the down curb. When you are sure of your position, praise the dog verbally, stroke the chin and give the dog kibble.

When crossing an intersection, handlers must listen to the rush of the parallel traffic. Contrary to some popular myths, the guide dog does not get cues from traffic lights; in fact, dogs cannot distinguish between green and red lights. It is up to the handler to determine when it is safe to cross. Once certain the parallel traffic is moving, the handler commands the dog forward. When the dog reaches the up curb it will stop. If the handler feels the dog slowing down during the crossing, the handler raises the strap and says "Curb."

As with curbs, the dogs also are trained to stop at the bottom and top of stairs.

If the dog leads the handler into an object like a trashcan, a pole or an overhanging branch, the handler should drop the harness, command the dog to sit and then tap the object with the hand or foot while saying; "Careful, careful." The handler then takes about five or ten steps back and commands the dog forward; this time the dog will stop at the object. The handler strokes the dog and rewards it with kibble. When a dog stops for a car blocking a driveway, the handler will command the dog to the street side and around the car and back to the sidewalk. Again, the dog is praised and given kibble. Food is the most effective tool in training and working guide dogs. I never go anywhere with my dog without a pocket or pouch full of kibble.

Now it was time for "Juno," a fictitious dog used by instructors to demonstrate the use of the leash and harness together. When I was in training, Juno was either a rolled-up carpet or a stuffed dog on wheels. That first time, Juno would be played by my instructor.

With my left hand, I firmly grabbed the handle of the harness as the instructor had demonstrated, slid the leash between my first and second fingers and commanded the instructor "Forward."

Using the roar of the traffic to my left as a cue, I continued straight ahead and stopped at the corner of Ludington and North. When I was sure the traffic to my left was moving, I crossed Ludington. After reaching the other side, I commanded Juno left and we continued down Ludington.

Juno veered onto someone's lawn—I corrected him with the "Hop up" command.

After the walk, we returned to my house, where the instructor conducted a one-hour interview. He assured me that I would be accepted into the guide dog program.

While I was in California, Donna would be left alone for twenty-eight days. She brought me out to the airport when it was time to leave for my training.

Donna grabbed me and wrapped her arms tightly around me.

"I love you so much and I'll miss you," she said tearfully.

"I'll call you every night," I promised.

A young man introduced himself to me and said he was to assist me. He led me up a ramp onto the plane and down a narrow aisle to my seat.

"Would you like the window?" asked the man seated to my left.

"Oh, no," I replied, smiling. "I'm blind."

During the flight before the stop-over in Denver, I tried napping, but I was too nervous. I kept thinking about catching the next flight to San Francisco and about San Rafael—I didn't know what to expect.

After we landed at Denver International, my assistant escorted me through the airport to the gate where I was to catch my flight to San Francisco. He took me to a waiting area where I handed my papers to the man behind the counter.

"It's flight 553 to San Francisco," I told the man. He assured me that someone would assist me when it was time to board.

"Remember," I repeated, "it's 553."

After I informed him that I was blind, he directed me to a soft chair near a wall.

As I sat down, I heard the voice of a woman to my right.

Wanting to make sure I wouldn't be left behind, I asked the woman to my right if she was going to San Francisco. She did not respond— she was engaged in a conversation with a young lady seated on her right. Then I heard a woman's voice over the PA announcing that they would be boarding flight 553 for San Francisco.

"That's my flight," I said. No one responded. "That's my flight!" I repeated loudly.

There I sat, squinting, listening—waiting to be called. Panic set in. "Are you on flight 553 for San Francisco? Is anyone around here?"

There was no response. Then I realized that there was no one around me—they were all on the plane. It was like one of those dreams I get where everyone around me disappears. Only this wasn't a dream. I sprung to my feet and started shouting.

A man came over and asked if he could assist me. When I told him about the flight, he took me over to the counter.

"This gentleman is supposed to be on flight 553."

"What's your name?"

"Philip DiMeo." I reached into my jacket and pulled out my papers; they were all crumpled.

"Philip DiMeo," he repeated.

"I'm blind and someone was supposed to take me on the plane."

"I can't find your name. Oh, here it is. This man will take you," he said.

Another man grabbed my arm, led me onto the plane and maneuvered me through the aisles to a seat.

"He can have the window," said a low-pitched female voice to my left.

"I don't need a window," I said.

"That's okay," she replied politely, "I really don't need the window."

"Neither do I—I'm blind."

The lady introduced herself. She was on her way to San Francisco to take a test for a real estate job. We made small talk until the flight attendant gave us our instructions—my seatmate helped me with my seat belt and oxygen mask.

Moments after takeoff, the woman next to me ordered a gin and tonic. I ordered coffee. After the drink she took me to the bathroom, waited and escorted me back to my seat. She munched on a bag of pretzels and ordered another gin and tonic. After the second drink, she became more friendly.

After landing in San Francisco, I was met by a man who persuaded me to sit in one of those airport wheelchairs. Suddenly, I heard a voice from behind shouting for me to be careful. It was my seatmate on the plane. Her warning clearly irritated the man; he muttered something I couldn't understand, then started pushing the wheelchair with me in it. My ex-seatmate, tagging behind, kept shouting for me to be careful—that infuriated the man to the point that he started to push faster; it was like a race between him and her while I hung onto the sides of the chair. While he took the corner, I heard my friend from the plane clopping behind.

She followed us all the way to the baggage claim area, which was my destination.

"Goodbye, Philip," she called out. "Good luck with your dog."

As I sat in that wheelchair, I wondered what was ahead. I wanted to get out of that wheelchair and walk somewhere, but where? Where was the person or persons who were supposed to meet me?

"Hi," a woman in a perky, high-pitched voice said. "I'm Clare—I will be your instructor."

This should be a lot of fun, I thought.

She took my arm and led me to a sofa where she introduced me to three of my soon-to-be classmates. There was a Catholic priest from San Diego, a 35-year-old lady who was also from San Diego and a 42-year-old self-described "gay radical" from Washington state.

Clare led us to the bus, seated us and passed out sandwiches and soft drinks. Clare drove through the Embarcadero and across the Golden Gate Bridge. She hummed and sang as she described the sights. It was evident that she really enjoyed what she was doing.

As she drove, she described the Frisco landmarks while I sat squinting. I saw nothing but glare. For all I knew, we could have been going across the 16th Street Viaduct in Milwaukee rather than the Golden Gate Bridge.

Clare took a wrong turn and we ended up in a traffic jam. She apologized for the delay and then went back to her singing. While we crept along, I heard the guy seated in front of me moaning. The sandwiches were too dry, the soft drinks weren't to his liking and the ride was too slow. To me, he seemed like a guy who demanded attention.

It was around 5:30 P.M. when we finally arrived at the San Rafael campus.

"Oh, I love this place," cried the thirty-five-year-old. "I don't want to ever go back home."

"When I call your name, come to the front of the bus," said Clare.

I sat quietly in the rear behind my teammates. My mind wandered, then I heard Clare's unmistakable voice.

"Okay Philip, walk to the front."

How many times would I hear that from her in the weeks to come?

After stepping off the bus, I turned to my right, listening to the familiar sound of those wooden canes scraping the pavement. Clare stood counting heads and then commanded us forward. I followed behind my teammates, carefully sliding my cane over the cracks along the grainy cement walkway.

"This will be your home for the next twenty-eight days," Clare said.

Then we stood silently while Clare described our surroundings.

"This is the San Rafael campus of Guide Dogs for the Blind. We are approximately twenty-five miles north of the Golden Gate Bridge. The campus is situated on eleven acres, surrounded by rolling hills with mountains in the background.

Across the road is the kennel with one hundred and fifty dogs. The dogs, bred on campus, are given to volunteer puppy raisers for training. After fourteen months, the puppy raisers return the dogs to the school for guide dog training. Most of you will meet your puppy raisers on the day of your graduation."

She then went on to describe our dorm: a one-story building with twelve rooms. As Clare spoke, I leaned against my cane and turned to the echoes of yelping puppies from the kennel across the road. *Maybe*, I thought, *one of those puppies will be my guide dog.*

Clare led us through the east entrance and into the hallway. I waited eagerly while she escorted my teammates to their rooms.

"Philip," she said, "follow me."

Dragging my cane against the cement corridor wall, I followed behind Clare. We walked about thirty paces and then stopped.

"This will be your room for the next twenty eight days. It is the fifth doorway from the entrance."

She grabbed my left hand and guided it to a smooth metal rectangle on the upper left side of the doorway. At the top of the rectangle was the room number in Braille below a large metal number 1 followed by the capitol letter A.

"This is your room, 1-A."

She led me through the doorway and described the room. To the left was a large plywood closet with two large doors that opened from the center. On the inside was a wooden rod extended between two walls with large metal hooks. To the left of that was a dresser with five drawers, a nightstand with a telephone and a bed. On the opposite wall were a vanity and a small bathroom. The other half of the room was what Clare described as a mirror image of my half.

"Your roommate is out on the veranda on the far wall next to the bed," she said. "If you need anything, please call me."

While fidgeting and cursing the maze of obnoxious zippers on the large suitcase that Donna had packed for me, I heard the shuffling of feet approaching. A man with a loud, deep voice introduced himself as my roommate, Jerry.

I extended my right hand but then stopped. *He's blind; he can't see it*, I thought. To my surprise, he wrapped his large hand around mine and we shook. Later, I discovered that he still had some of his sight. Jerry explained that he was in the initial stages of macular degeneration and wanted a guide dog before he lost all of his sight.

Soon I discovered that even though all the students were legally blind, my roommate wasn't the only member of the class who was partially sighted. Out of a class of eleven, only three of us were completely blind.

Clare led us into the dining room for our 6:30 P.M. dinner. We were each assigned to a specific table and sat in a specific chair. There were place cards with our names printed on them. Seated with me were three teammates. One guy and I made small talk while the women sat silently.

The man I was speaking with was born with what he described as cancer in his right eye. Despite losing sight in that eye, he was able to play goalie on a hockey team. In 2002, he developed cancer in the left eye. With the spreading of the cancer, the pain became unbearable. Not even morphine could alleviate the excruciating pain.

"I was on every kind of painkiller you could imagine," he said. "Nothing worked. It was either having the sight in my left eye and enduring the pain or eliminating the pain and losing my vision. I chose the latter."

After the meal, I returned to the room and unpacked while my roommate explored the facility. Seated at the table, I familiarized myself with the phone; specifically, the zillions of buttons. Then I called Donna. We talked for about twenty minutes. I told her again that I would call her every day, whenever I had downtime.

My roommate returned to the room at about 8 P.M. He told me that he was retired and lived in a large house on a seventeen-acre ranch in California.

"We have horses, cows, chickens, dogs, cats and ducks. We have a river that runs through our place and the cats are always dragging water snakes into the house. Tarantulas are frequent visitors to our house," he said, laughing.

Since we shared the bathroom, I agreed to shower at night to allow him his morning shower. As we sat talking, I heard the echoing sounds of white canes tapping their way along the hallway floor.

"I'm a quiet sleeper," he said. "You don't have to worry about me snoring."

Unfortunately, Jerry had never heard himself sleep, because he actually did snore; he snored *very* loudly.

The next morning we stood in line next to the open cafeteria doorway. I didn't know if I was in the right place until I heard the rattling of trays. One of the kitchen staff rang the chimes—the signal for us to tap our way to our tables. My table was easy to find: it was the first table to the right of the door.

Each morning, the kitchen staff alternated hot cereals followed by eggs, muffins, pancakes and sausage. I stuck to the hot cereal and toast; the others had the hot cereal and whatever else they were serving.

At 8:00 A.M., we attended our first of many lectures in the plush Dayroom.

Clare set the tone. "This is not a vacation," Clare barked at someone who was five minutes late. Then Clare welcomed us to Guide Dogs for the Blind, introduced us to the other instructors and gave us a brief history of the school.

"You are class 649," she said proudly. Then she spoke of our schedule.

"Lectures are at 8:00 A.M. sharp, not 8:05 or 8:01. Anyone who is tardy for three lectures will be bounced from the program."

Clare then asked us to introduce ourselves.

I introduced myself as a "cheese-head" from Wauwatosa, Wisconsin who had coached the greatest co-ed softball team in Milwaukee history.

Clare thanked us for coming and went through the code of conduct: "No smoking in the dorm, no drinking liquor in the dorm, no leaving the dorm with your dogs, no mistreating the dogs, no gambling with classmates, no fighting with classmates and no having sex with classmates."

"How about with the dogs?" I quipped.

Everyone laughed—at least I thought everyone laughed until several days later, when I was summoned into Clare's office for making inappropriate comments.

On our first official day of training, at 9:00 A.M. we learned about guide and obedience commands and about the collar, leash and harness. At 9:30, we attached a rig to the fictitious dog, Juno, a rolled-up carpet or a stuffed dog on wheels.

Clare provided the sound effects for my first experience with Juno. She whimpered, sniffed and barked while I attached the leash and harness to the rug. She tugged the rug from the front and I commanded her to move forward. She barked, panted and even growled at the other rolled-up rugs maneuvering down the hallway.

At 9:30, we boarded the bus to the downtown lounge. "This will be your home away from home," said Clare. To the right of the entrance was a kitchenette with a stove, refrigerator, microwave and coffee maker. Across the aisle were the Music Room and the main lounge. The rooms were carpeted and furnished with soft chairs and couches.

On the second day, we graduated from rolled-up carpets to practice with real dogs—mine was named Calvin, a feisty fifteen-month-old black Labrador from the kennel across the yard. Like me, he was still in training. He nudged me, pawed me and licked me—I wanted to take him home. I commanded Calvin to shake hands like he was my pet. Clare gently reprimanded me and pointed out that a guide dog was not a pet, but a trusted companion.

It did not take me long to realize that we were being trained the same as the dogs. When we messed up, we were verbally reprimanded, their way of giving us a correction, and when we did well, we were complimented with phrases such as "Real good, Phil, real good" or "Atta boy, atta boy, Phil." All that was missing was the stroking of the chin and a piece of kibble.

Wednesday, October 13 was the big day, the day we were to be presented with our dogs for the course. We would be receiving the dogs in our rooms at around 2:00 P.M., Clare told us at the morning lecture. We had no idea of what the dogs would be like except that they would be Labs.

"Philip," Clare said, raising her voice, "your dog is Cliff, a male black Labrador, twenty-two inches and weighing seventy pounds. Cliff will be two years old on October 14, which is tomorrow."

It seemed like forever waiting for Clare to bring Cliff but she finally arrived at 2:30.

"Here you are, Phil," she said, pushing the dog's strap into my hand.

His tail was wagging. He licked my hands and pushed his large body into my legs. His head nudged me and he kissed me when I bent over. He put his head on the floor with his butt up in the air.

I kept Cliff on a short leash while he tugged and nudged me. We played for about twenty minutes, then I tethered him to the cable next to the wall. The difficult part was yet to come. Along with intense training, Cliff had to be cared for. First, there was the feeding; a cup and a half of dog food with a half cup of water at 6:15 A.M., relieving at 6:30, relieving at 9:00, water and relieving at 11:45, relieving after the 1:30 P.M. lecture, feed, water and relieve at 4:45, water at 7:00 and final relieving at 9:00.

We were given a fanny pack, a small travel bag with zippered compartments. Inside was a "zoom groom," a small circular device with rubber spikes used to massage the dog's neck and back, a zip brush for stroking the dog and a plastic comb. The fanny pack also contained a small tube of poultry-flavored toothpaste with a rubber device shaped like a toothbrush that went over the index finger.

During downtime that evening, I called Donna and told her about my new dog.

When I wasn't working him, I took Cliff to the music room, the computer room and the workout room. While others left the campus with their weekend visitors, Cliff and I spent our first Sunday walking and listening to the radio broadcast of the Green Bay Packers game.

Chapter 15

Goodbye Cliff, Hello Ladonna

It was 5:30 A.M., the voice on my watch said. Carefully, I slipped out of bed and made my way to the bathroom, not wanting to wake up my roommate. Even with the door closed, I could still hear Jerry snoring like a buzz saw. While I did my business, Cliff was curled up on his fleece mat, probably watching me.

After shaving, I grabbed Cliff's metal dish, stepped out of my room and headed for the kennel kitchen. Directly across the hallway from my room, the kennel kitchen was a small room with a metal sink, a large wooden table, some cabinets and a large bin of dog food.

After I had bumped into some people already waiting in line, the partially-sighted Father Greg grabbed my arm and assisted me to the back of the line. One by one, the group stepped into the room, scooped up the kibble with a plastic cup and dumped it into the doggie dish. The clicking of kibble hitting the metal dishes stirred up the dogs tethered in the rooms. Some whined, some moaned and a few yelped—I hoped it wasn't Cliff yelping.

Cliff gulped down his breakfast, banging the metal dish against the wall, then dove into the water bowl I had placed on the floor under the sink. Cliff attacked the bowl of water the same way he attacked his food. Suddenly, I heard the bowl clang against the wall and felt water streaming over my shoe.

After wiping the floor with a bathroom towel, I headed for the loading dock. Again, I bumped into one of my classmates and another steered me to the back of the line.

We stood waiting for Clare to shout out instructions. When she called my name, I grabbed Cliff's harness and walked to the sound of her voice. She directed me to the curb and told me to stop.

"Where's your hand, Phil?" she asked.

"What do you mean?"

Clare clopped toward me. She grabbed my left hand and pressed my thumb against a small leather ridge.

"Always put your thumb on the nubbin. The nubbin!" she repeated. "Now go back to the door and try it again."

So, again, I heeled Cliff to my side and walked back to the door.

The next morning at breakfast, Cliff became fidgety and lunged at my teammate's dog. A correction, a slight jerk of the leash, was all Cliff needed.

On Thursday, after obedience training, we had our first workout on the obstacle course. The dogs were to take us around a slight curve and to the top of seven brick steps. When the dog stopped, we were to feel for the edge of the step with our left foot and then command the dog forward down the steps. At the bottom was the obstacle course, a narrow winding cement pathway with objects meant to distract the dogs.

"Left Phil, left, turn!" Clare shouted when Cliff led me into the maintenance area. "Feel the domes, then turn," she shouted. "Now do it over. Stop!" she shouted. "Do you know where you are, mister? You have to be aware of where you are."

The partially sighted people had no trouble with the course—they simply led their dogs around the turns and onto the busses. From there we headed for the lounge in downtown San Rafael to continue working the dogs.

The next task seemed simple enough—just walk toward the sound of the traffic—what could go wrong?

First, I made sure I was at the door. With left foot forward, I commanded Cliff toward the sound of traffic. With each step, however, I became apprehensive; I feared walking into the street. I halted Cliff about five or six feet from the curb.

"What are you doing?" Clare warned from my left. "Reach for the curb with your left foot."

I probed with my left foot but couldn't locate the curb.

"Well, are you by the curb?" Clare called.

"I think so."

"No, you are not. You're a couple feet away—tell Cliff to hop up."

I commanded Cliff and he moved forward.

"Reach out now."

I slid my left foot forward and finally felt a gentle slope.

Except for feeding and relieving our dogs, Sunday was our day off. Since I had no visitors, my Sundays were spent hanging out with Cliff. We took short walks, listened to football on the radio and played in our room.

Because of the hectic training schedule, it was difficult to find time to work out at Guide Dogs for the Blind. Donna and I were up at dawn and on our exercise equipment at the YMCA by 5:15

A.M. While in training, I could only work out during downtime; that is, time when we were not in lectures or working our dogs. I usually worked out during the noon lunch hour or when not on night routes at 7:00 P.M. Unlike the Y, the dorm workout room down the hallway had just a few pieces of equipment from which to choose. Along with a hot and cold water dispenser and a refrigerator there was a treadmill, a recumbent bike, a combination bike/rowing machine and a set of light dumbbells. For my workout, I chose the combination bike/rowing machine.

At first, I took Cliff with me and tethered him to a cable attached to the wall next to the dumbbells. While I worked out, Cliff usually sprawled out on the rug and slept. One evening while I was a half-hour into my workout I heard Cliff chewing on something but did not investigate. Jerry, who was at the hot water dispenser, started shouting at me.

"Look what your dog did!" he yelled.

Since I was not sighted, I had no idea what he was talking about. Emphatically, he told me that Cliff had chewed through the plastic coating on those dumbbells. The carpet near the dumbbells was covered with blue shavings.

"You have to watch your dog. It's your fault. He could develop serious stomach problems and die. We'll have to monitor his stool."

Luckily, Cliff was fine, but I knew I had to monitor him more closely.

We continued training with our dogs every day.

For me, it was difficult to tell where the downward slope of the down curb ended and the road began. Several times Cliff did not stop for the down curb and Clare, clopping behind, called me on it.

"Make sure you know where the curb is," she reminded me.

Cliff ran a curb on E Street and veered toward the parallel traffic. Clare immediately grabbed my arm and steered me back. "Cliff wouldn't let you get hit by a car," she said.

"I'm glad *you* think so." I wasn't so sure.

Friday, October 15, was the day of our class picture. We met in the Dayroom for a brief lecture and then returned to our rooms to dress up for the photo. My outfit consisted of a dark shirt, dark dress pants and a gray sweater vest. I found everything but the one pair of dark dress socks. "I'll pull my pant legs over my ankles and no one will know I'm wearing white socks," I said to Cliff as he relaxed on his fleece mat.

We assembled in the music room and were led to the graduation stage for the class photo. I sat on the second row of bleachers between Stacy, a female classmate and Father Greg. I tried to keep my knees down, hoping my pants would cover the white socks. In order to get the dogs' attention, the photographer squeezed a rubber toy, yelped, whimpered and barked.

After the class photo, we were led back to the music room for ID photos with our dogs. I sat on a chair in front of a screen with Cliff to my left.

While everyone went to lunch, I took Cliff to the veranda for grooming. After zoom grooming, brushing and combing, I was ready to brush his teeth for the first time. Cliff sat wagging his tail while I smeared the poultry-flavored toothpaste onto a rubber finger puppet. Gently, I closed Cliff's mouth, found his teeth and stroked from left to right. After returning to the room, I discovered that the cap for the toothpaste was missing. I returned to the veranda and groped the cement floor, sweeping back and forth with my left hand, crawling on my hands and knees. I found the cap alright, except it was all chewed up.

During the second week, the re-trainees, those people who had had guide dogs before, arrived. Since they were experienced, they required only three weeks of training instead of the four weeks that new trainees got.

Unlike our class, all eight re-trainees were totally blind. On Wednesday, October 20, we were taken to the downtown lounge for route training. We assembled in the music room where Clare introduced us to the basic route; down 4th Street to E Street. Cross E, stop, turn right and cross 4th, continue down E to 3rd Street, left on 3rd to D, left on D to 4th, 4th to E, cross E, stop, turn right, cross 4th, stop, turn left and back to the lounge.

Some of us were confused and most were nervous, but Jessie, one teammate born sightless, was terrified.

"The route is in the shape of the letter P," Clare said.

"I don't know what P looks like," pleaded Jessie. "I was born without sight—I can't visualize any letters, shapes or streets."

Cliff and I walked toward the sound of the perpendicular traffic, stopped and turned left. Clare said nothing. *That was good*, I thought. It meant that I hadn't screwed up. A couple of times the harness tugged, which meant that Cliff was going too fast. I steadied him and continued with Clare clopping behind. I concentrated on my mechanics, making sure my feet were positioned to alert Cliff when I would be continuing straight ahead or turning right or left. With the offset, I didn't have to worry about bumping Cliff.

Everything went smoothly until we crossed E Street. After commanding Cliff forward, I felt as if we were going uphill instead of down. Suddenly, I was in an enclosed area with a large metal door directly in front of me. Clare, shouting from behind, informed me that I had walked into a building. Apparently, I had steered Cliff too far to the left.

We reworked the route and continued down E Street. We worked G Street and 2nd Street with no problems. On 3rd Street, however, Cliff started tugging and pulling me to the left.

"He's going to poop," Clare advised. "Remove his harness."

After halting Cliff, Clare led us to a grassy area. Cliff sniffed, danced and did his business. Clare, who always came prepared, pulled out a plastic bag from her pocket and retrieved Cliff's droppings.

Halfway down D Street, Cliff started tugging. He quickened his pace and his tail was wagging. *Dog distraction*, I thought. I pulled on his harness. Cliff kept tugging and veered to his left. First I gave him a slight correction; that didn't work. Upon Clare's insistence, I resorted to the "base-ball correction"—grabbing the leash with both hands like a baseball bat and yanking upward. That steadied him.

When we returned to the lounge, Clare praised me. She told me I was doing a great job.

The next morning we went to Civic Center Park for dog distractions. Civic Center Park was noted for an assortment of birds which included ducks, geese and seagulls. We were to start off with obedience commands and walk the dogs along the edge of a large pond, an exercise to determine how the dogs would react to bird distractions. While the group was at the pond, my supervisor, Jason, took me to a grassy area to see if we could get Cliff to do his business, mainly "number two." We stood out there for what seemed like an hour walking around in circles but Cliff did not respond. He sniffed and chewed grass and leaves, but would not poop. I also tried to do some obedience practice with Cliff but he wouldn't obey, so I returned to the bus.

Cliff was causing me more and more trouble and couldn't seem to follow the guide rules. I was worried but I knew being dropped from the guide program wasn't the end of the line for service dogs. Many of the dogs do make career changes. Some are service dogs for the physically handicapped or those in wheelchairs. Some become police dogs, some are used as bomb sniffing dogs, some are trained for the military and some become great pets.

Cliff and I were having roadblocks working together at times. For example, one morning everything was going smoothly until we reached 3rd Street. Halfway down the block, I felt Cliff pulling to the left yet again. The supervisor recommended and I finally decided, despite my fondness for Cliff, that I would make a switch of guide dogs while I still had some training time left.

When we went back to our room that day, Cliff came up to me and kept nudging me—he wanted to play. I didn't feel like playing with Cliff. I pulled him toward me—there was a lump in my throat. I lowered myself to the floor and hugged him. Again, he nudged me with his head and licked my left cheek.

"Phil," my supervisor called from the hallway. "Come into my office. Leave Cliff here."

This was it. I led Cliff around the bed and tethered him to the wall, then knelt and gave him one last hug. He licked my hand and sprawled out on his fleece mat. There I stood, motionless; frozen to the floor. I didn't want to leave. Tearfully, I looked down to where Cliff was.

"So long, Cliff," I said softly. I walked to the door, grabbed my cane and stepped into the hallway.

My supervisor again said I'd made a wise decision. I told him I was ready. According to him, there were two dogs available for me; Fait and Ladonna, both female yellow Labradors. He recommended Ladonna but told me I could work both dogs and choose.

"You recommend Ladonna?" I asked.

"For you, Phil," he replied, "Ladonna will be perfect."

I chose Ladonna.

"You have made a wise choice," the supervisor nodded.

He told me that Cliff would be taken back to the kennel and would either be re-trained or become someone's pet. He asked if I wanted to say goodbye to Cliff and I said no. I just couldn't.

"Will my new dog have any of the problems that Cliff had?" I wondered.

"Ladonna is wonderful," the supervisor responded.

After he left the room, I sat fidgeting with my cane. My stomach was in knots. I felt guilty about Cliff. I wanted so much to take him home, but I had to have a dog whom I could trust. After fifteen minutes, the supervisor returned with my new dog. The puppy rubbed against me, danced, turned her butt toward me and lay on the floor, waiting for me to rub her belly. I couldn't help smiling.

The supervisor described Ladonna as a yellow Lab with a creamy coat speckled with red. Her ears were honey colored. Her eyes were brown with brown markings which looked like eyeliner. She was seventeen months old, twenty-one inches tall and weighed fifty-nine pounds.

Cliff was gone when Ladonna and I returned to the room. All that was left as a remembrance of Cliff was his fleece mat, which would now be Ladonna's. She walked over to it, sniffed it and then lay down. After tethering Ladonna, I telephoned Donna to tell her I had finally been paired with the perfect companion.

"You'll never guess what my new dog's name is," I teased.

At our next 1:30 P.M. lecture, I introduced Ladonna to the class. They were all curious as to how I felt after losing Cliff. Giving up Cliff was a difficult decision to make, I told them; I was sad about Cliff but happy with Ladonna, who quickly made friends with everyone.

Chapter 16

Practice Makes Perfect

There were only two weeks left and Ladonna and I had tons of information to learn, our supervisor said. Along with working the basic routes, there would be freelancing and night routes on Tuesdays and Thursdays.

"Why night routes?" asked one member of our group.

"That's for another meeting," Clare said.

While she spoke, Ladonna turned and thumped her tail.

"Yeow, yeow!" something screeched.

Ladonna reared to her left. Two dogs from the couch growled and then started barking. "Heel your dogs!" shouted Clare.

While the room seemed to be in chaos, I heeled Ladonna and commanded her down.

"That's what you call a cat distraction," laughed one of my teammates.

Apparently, one of the nurses had brought her large cat into the room and had run it through the unsuspecting dogs.

"That cat looks more like a dog," said another from my left.

"It's really a dog in a cat's body," joked my supervisor.

The nurse had adopted the cat after it was seriously injured and trained it like a dog. She kept the large cat on a training leash and walked it around the campus.

Unlike the other dogs, Ladonna was not spooked by the large cat or the other dogs. She was—and still is—laid back. During dog or cat distractions, she wagged her tail and sniffed—living up to the "Miss Congeniality" title given to her by her puppy raisers in Arizona.

After class, we took the dogs to the kennel for obedience training. Along the cement walls were large metal crates with yelping puppies. Ladonna's head moved from left to right while her tail rapidly thumped my left leg. We stopped in the middle of one hallway for obedience commands. She responded well; I rewarded her with kibble, a practice that continues to this day.

Since there were only two weeks of training left, I had to work Ladonna twice as hard; I had to make up for the first two weeks when I had Cliff. While the others did freelancing (picking a specific route or destination like the coffee shop or pet store), Clare took Ladonna and I on the traffic route, which I had practiced with Cliff the previous week. Ladonna performed well. She stopped for cars blocking the sidewalk and backed me up when a moving car approached. Nevertheless, I told Clare that I felt I was too far to the right.

"It could be the offset," she said. "We'll see if you should go back to the regular harness."

When we returned to the lounge, Clare said she wanted me to work Ladonna on the basic route. *That would be better than sitting around*, I thought. Besides, with only about two weeks left, I needed as much work with Ladonna as I could get.

Ladonna was smooth and walked fast, but after my experience with Cliff I still didn't fully trust her. I always halted her a few feet from the down curb.

"Go all the way to the curb, Phil," Clare insisted.

On the way back to the lounge, I brushed against a building to my right.

"I'll see about getting you a regular harness," Clare said.

At 1:30 P.M., we met in the Dayroom, received instructions from Clare and went through the obstacle course. Ladonna led me down the steps, around the domes and to the bus. At the down-town lounge I sat talking with another teammate until Clare called me. Since it was freelancing and I could pick my route, I chose the basic one.

Ladonna and I took off toward E Street with Clare clopping behind in her large boots. I was elated when we had no trouble executing stops and turns—Ladonna was perfect. As we walked, my confidence in Ladonna grew. We continued down 4th Street, down E to 3rd and up to D. We crossed D and hastened the pace down 4th. We continued at a fast, steady pace until we reached the middle of the block where she ran me into a metal pole. I was dazed. The right side of my face from my forehead to my chin was stinging and the inside of my mouth was bleeding.

"I think I lost a tooth," I said, spitting out blood.

"It was your fault, not hers," Clare shouted from behind. "It was your fault. You led her into the pole."

"I lost a tooth."

"You have to correct her and rework the route."

"I lost a tooth and you want me to rework the route?"

"Are you all right?"

I felt my mouth and found all my teeth were still there. After heeling Ladonna, we re-worked the route; this time Ladonna took me safely around the pole.

"Praise her. Give her some strokes and some kibble," Clare said.

I wasn't quite ready to do that, but I tried.

"Good girl," I said, giving her some kibble.

In truth, I was frustrated; my head was bruised and my mouth was bloody and swollen. I was about to give up trying to train a guide dog and instead return to the dreaded white cane.

Later, Clare stopped into my room to see how I felt. She told me she was sorry; she hadn't thought I would walk into the pole.

"If I would have seen it I would have stopped you," she said.

I nodded but said nothing.

At 7:30 P.M. we assembled in the Dayroom for our first night route.

"I can't see very well at night," one teammate moaned.

"Welcome to the club," I whispered to the guy seated to my right.

We started in the foyer and then did the obstacle course to the busses. Ladonna and I boarded bus number two and I took my customary seat.

"I don't see why we have to go on night routes," whined another teammate. "I never go out at night. I'm not going to take Wilbur out at night."

"This is awful," groaned another.

"It's just as bad for the instructors," I pointed out.

After boarding the bus and counting heads, Clare told us that we were going to a specific street from which we would have to find our way back to the lounge. She also told us that the re-trainees would be doing the route as well and they would go first. Two teammates, sitting in the rear of the bus, kept complaining about doing the night route. I personally was upset about the eight re-trainees going ahead of us. Why couldn't they have gone on another night?

We sat intently while Clare gave us our instructions. We were to get off the bus, stop and face the front. At her command, we were to walk forward to the next street and stop. While she spoke, I heard two of the women moaning softly.

"You cross E and keep going," Clare continued, "until you get to the next street, that's F. You go to the curb, stop, make a right and continue down F until you get to the next street, 4th. Cross 4th, stop, make a right and continue until you get to the lounge."

I pictured the route in my head. We were entering the lounge from the opposite direction of the basic route. Clare repeated the route several times. One woman was breathing hard and another kept complaining about how she had trouble seeing at night.

Clare said we were to go in three-minute intervals and one guy agreed to keep time. Since I dislike waiting around, I volunteered to go first.

Clare called me forward and our timekeeper pressed his watch; it was 8:13 P.M. I stepped off the bus and turned to my left. "Ladonna, forward," I commanded. *This time*, I thought, *my mechanics have to be perfect*, and I was going to make sure they were. Since I had switched back to a normal harness without an offset, there would be no walking into objects to my right.

As we started, I caught some glare and heard the sounds of oncoming traffic to my left. We reached the first intersection and Ladonna came to a smooth stop. I probed with my left foot and sure enough, it was the down curb.

"Good girl, Ladonna," I said, stroking her chin. I listened for the roar of traffic but heard nothing.

"It's all clear, Phil," said an instructor from the re-trainee class.

We started across E when I felt a tug to my right shoulder. "She's leading you too far to the left," the instructor said. "Correct her."

I gave Ladonna a tug to the right and a hop up command. She led me to the up curb and we continued. The rest of the route was perfect. She made the moving turn on 4th Street and led me to the lounge. Ladonna and I joined the other re-trainees, who were seated along the patio wall. We talked for a while until the instructor summoned them onto the bus. After thanking the instructor for rescuing me from the traffic, I joined two teammates in the music room. One was upset about the night route and the other was upset that he had missed the ballgame.

It was around 10:00 P.M. when I took Ladonna to the relieving area. Obediently she did her business. All I wanted was to get back to the room and crawl into bed.

After the morning meeting the next day, we did the usual obedience training, the obstacle course and boarded the busses; our destination was San Francisco. Everyone was excited. Clare drove with the radio blasting.

"How's Ladonna working out?" my instructor asked.

"Great."

"Good. You made a good choice, Phil."

The roads were worn and the ride was bumpy but we managed to reach San Francisco in an hour. Clare first took us to Chestnut Street to begin the workout. Along with working sidewalk and street routes, we were to ride a city bus. With my instructor as my guide, we boarded a bus somewhere on Chestnut and rode for about seven blocks. We sat in the front, the area designated for the handicapped. From the bus we worked our way back to the van. He described the area as we walked—large buildings, shops and restaurants.

On the walk back, he led me to the bus, which was empty.

While the instructor left to join the other students, I curled up for some much-needed sleep on the large seat at the rear.

After my nap, we went down several steep hills and crossed some busy intersections. It was exciting, especially walking across the historic cable car tracks. Although I couldn't see San Francisco, I could sure feel it. Crowds of people cut between and in front of us. Though it was noisy and chaotic, the chaos did not affect Ladonna. We crossed an intersection with a grassy island. Ladonna took me around the grassy area and stopped at the downcurb. From there we went down several flights of steps to the subway area. We continued walking through Union Square. Clare described the area and the people.

Ladonna kept her focus while leading me through a crowd picketing a hotel. When we returned to the bus, Clare praised me. Ladonna and I had had a good morning.

I felt Ladonna and I were becoming a team. The more we worked, the more confident of her I became. Even her main problem, that she walked me too close to objects to my right, was correctable. Each time I brushed a bush, a pole or the side of a building as I did on E-Street, I stopped, gave her a correction and re-worked the route.

As my satisfaction and confidence grew with Ladonna, I was impressed with the instruction I was getting. I told her and the instructor to let me know when I made a mistake. "I want to leave all my mistakes in San Rafael, so when I screw up I want you to jump all over me," I said.

"You can be sure of that," said Clare.

Much to the displeasure of the class, we went out on another night route that evening. This time, however, it was without the re-trainees.

Clare drove to an area about four blocks from the lounge and gave directions. The route was similar to the basic route. As usual, I went first. I was confident. The regular harness was working out and Ladonna and I were working well together.

Ladonna took me to the first street and then stopped for the down curb. We continued two blocks and made a right turn. *So far, so good,* I thought. The instructors were stationed at every crossing—I could hear their walkie-talkies. We made our second right turn. Unfortunately, Ladonna became distracted by a large crack in the pavement. She stopped. I probed with my left foot and assumed we were at a down curb. I commanded her left. Before I realized what was happening, I was in the middle of the road. Fortunately, the instructor saw me and led me to the sidewalk. Normally, I could determine where I was by the sound of the traffic, but at that time of the night, no traffic was on the street. I became frustrated and lost my concentration. I halted Ladonna four feet from the down curb on 4th Street. Sensing my frustration, the instructor following behind told me that I was doing well.

"I'm not," I said, feeling down.

"Just remember the basics," he said. "Remember the basics and you'll be fine."

On Friday, our new destination was Berkeley College. We had a choice of working the dogs on campus or in the neighborhood; I chose the neighborhood. Ladonna performed well with the exception of leading me toward a trashcan. I corrected her and reworked the route. Clare was pleased with my progress, she said, specifically my footwork.

On the way back to the bus, I felt a strong tug on the harness—I was being pulled to the left. At first, I thought Ladonna had become distracted and had veered off the sidewalk. *She must be a lot stronger than I realized*, I thought. Clare shouted for me to give Ladonna a correction to the right. When we returned to the bus, Clare told me that a homeless man had grabbed Ladonna's harness and tried to rip it off.

The majority of the afternoon was spent freelancing from the lounge. For my route, I chose a store two and a half blocks from the lounge and a straight shot down 4th Street. We crossed E and D. There was the store, the fourth building to the left. I walked twenty paces and made a moving left turn. "Next door," Clare yelled from behind. I found the door and heeled Ladonna into the store. Clare followed.

"Do I get any freebies?" I asked.

"I'm afraid not," laughed Clare.

The following Saturday morning, we did a sidewalk-less route in a rural area. It was warm and breezy, a perfect day for a walk in the country. While we walked, the instructor described the surroundings; open areas of yellowish short grass, rolling hills and few trees. To me it was like out of a western movie. I pictured cowboys riding over the hills and across the open areas. For so many years I had wanted to go to California; I had fantasized about being in an area like that and I was finally there, but without sight. It frustrated me not to be able to see the scenery. At noon, the instructors treated us to lunch at a Mexican restaurant in San Rafael.

We talked about graduation. Only one more week left and we would be returning home with our dogs. Some teammates had already started packing. One was melancholy; she wanted to stay in San Rafael—she did not want to leave.

Although I was anxious to go home, I told them I was going to enjoy and experience my last week in San Rafael. Who knew if I would ever be back there again? I was especially looking forward to taking Ladonna on our scheduled trip to the redwood forest at Muir Woods National Monument.

Chapter 17

Graduation

The mood at our Monday morning meeting was more upbeat than it had been since we arrived—Clare told us that we were all graduating.

"Everyone will be able to go home with their dogs," she revealed. It was a tremendous relief for all of us.

This was finally our last week, a week of fun. There would be Fisherman's Wharf, the San Francisco airport and the redwood forest. There was also apprehension, the challenge route and self-orientation. Self-orientation worried me. Unlike the basic route or freelancing, self-orientation meant that each of us would be dropped in an unknown location and would have to make our way back to the downtown lounge. It seemed like fun to two classmates, whose vision allowed them to navigate without relying on their dogs. To those of us without sight, it was just plain scary.

We started the morning on the obstacle course, then worked our dogs at the kennel for obedience training and the weigh-in. The instructors stressed the importance of maintaining the dog's weight, particularly explaining the problems of overweight dogs. Labs can be eating machines, Clare said. If not checked, the dog will eat itself right out of a job. Problems with overweight dogs usually occur after graduation, when the students return home with their dogs. Some dogs may gain as much as thirty pounds. Clare told us of a graduate who, every morning, took his dog to a doughnut shop for breakfast. While sitting at the counter eating his pastry, he was unaware that some guy was slipping chocolate and cream-filled doughnuts to his dog. The dog, originally eighty pounds when he first started getting the treats, ballooned to a whopping one hundred and fifty pounds; nearly twice his original weight. Consequently, that dog was returned to the school and retired.

At the lounge, we freelanced; I did a modified version of the basic route—I extended the route two blocks. I walked Ladonna as if I was back in Milwaukee, pretending I was working Milwaukee and Cherry Streets, the streets surrounding the Schlitz Building. The more we walked, the more confident I became. Unlike Cliff, who I had to direct, Ladonna was, as the instructor said, quick to make decisions. After stopping at every street crossing, her head rotated from side to side, sizing up the situation, then waiting for my command whether to turn left or right or continue straight ahead.

That afternoon was the challenge route. We would be dropped off on a designated street corner from which we had to make it back to the lounge. We were given the choice of how far we wanted to walk—short, medium or long. My two classmates without sight chose the shortest route; I decided to take my chances with the longest route, two miles from the lounge.

The route was simple but full of distractions. There were sidewalk cafes, parking lots, sidewalk food vendors and, of course, other dogs.

It was a gorgeous day, warm and sunny with a slight breeze. I was full of confidence. I concentrated on the basics as my supervisor had stressed. The oncoming traffic to my right would be the best indicator of where I was. We crossed two streets and turned right. *So far, so good*, I thought. However, something happened on the third block. The harness tugged to the left—somehow I was walking up a slight incline; it certainly wasn't the sidewalk.

"You're on a ramp!" the instructor shouted. "Let her guide you around it."

On the next block, Ladonna led me into a table. The chatter of people and the smell told me Ladonna had veered me into one of those sidewalk cafes—two blocks later, it was a parking lot. I recovered and then rendezvoused with the other bus at the halfway point.

After a break, Ladonna and I returned to my room. Clare had asked me to meet with her. It was time for my mid-week evaluation. Although there was no reason to be nervous, I was. I tethered Ladonna, grabbed my cane and headed toward the main office.

Clare said I had done exceptionally well and told me I had the best attitude in the class. My instructor also praised me for what he called "going the extra mile" when Cliff didn't work out and I had to start again with Ladonna.

Since they were throwing praise around, I threw some back at them. I told them I thought I was getting the finest instruction in the country.

"It was a pleasure having you in the class," my instructor said. Clare agreed.

Both our class and the re-trainees attended the 1:30 P.M. meeting. Julie, a graduate of Guide Dogs for the Blind, lectured us on what to expect when we returned home with our dogs. I still recall her emphasizing the image we were to promote, that of a competent, compassionate guide dog handler.

The thought of returning home both excited and worried me. Would I be ready? Only four more days left and I wanted to make sure I was ready to face the world with Ladonna. I talked to her, praising her at every down curb. After every route, I praised her and gave her kibble.

On Tuesday we boarded the busses and headed for Fisherman's Wharf—everyone was bubbly. Clare sang while driving. When we arrived at Fisherman's Wharf, I stepped off the bus and strolled for about fifteen minutes. Ladonna led me to a café where I ordered a large hazelnut coffee.

At Fisherman's Wharf, my plan was to buy some souvenirs for the family. And since the Wharf was a historical site, I would have my picture taken.

Clare took me on a short route and described the area, including the landmarks. We crossed several streets then stopped for photos. Next she took me to a flea market where I bought T-shirts for my daughters and sweatshirts for my wife and son.

We all got back on the bus. Four blocks from the lounge, the bus stopped.

"All right, gang," Clare said. "You are going to go first." Clare gave us the route. "You are to leave at three minute intervals." I volunteered to go first. This was the last night route and I wanted it to be perfect—no mistakes this time.

With Ladonna properly positioned to my left, I walked to the corner and then stopped, waiting for the sound of the traffic. It was quiet, not a truck, bus or car to be heard.

We crossed, stopped at the up curb and continued. When we reached the next intersection, however, Ladonna did not stop. By the time I had realized what had happened we were on the other side of the street. We went back about twenty paces and reworked the route. This time Ladonna stopped at the curb; I slipped her a kibble.

It was after 11:00 P.M. when I crawled into bed. I reached down and groped. She was lying on her fleece mat alongside chewed-up balls of yarn. After pulling up my covers, I discovered that Ladonna had somehow chewed up almost half of the quilting of the bedspread.

The re-trainees joined us at the 8:00 A.M. meeting. One of the re-trainee instructors, who had trained Ladonna, led us out onto the graduate stage where we went through obedience training.

On Thursday, I had my exit interview with the CEO of Guide Dogs for the Blind. The interview was our chance to rate the program and offer suggestions to improve the training that we had received. He asked me several questions with which he wanted me to evaluate the program on a scale of 1 to 5. I rated everything as a 5, from the training and food to the facilities. I told him I was especially impressed with my supervisor and instructor. He told me that he had heard from the instructors that I had the best attitude of any student in our class.

Later, we boarded the bus for Civic Center Park for more bird distractions.

How would Ladonna react to the bird distractions? We walked around the pond listening to the birds, ducks, geese and whatever else was flying or swimming. Ladonna kept her focus; she was not distracted in any way.

We were an apprehensive group at the self-orientation meeting. Even those with sight were anxious.

"Listen up, gang," Clare said. "We will drop each of you off at a specific street in downtown San Rafael. It will be an area that you have worked before. We will tell you what street you are on and you will have to find your way back to the lounge. If you are lost, you can ask a pedestrian."

"What if there's no one around?" one teammate asked.

"Drop your harness and stand there and one of us will help you. We will be stationed at different corners."

I heeled Ladonna and walked to the steps. We stepped off the bus where the instructor was waiting.

"Okay Phil," he said. He told me I was on the corner of some street I had never heard of. I then asked about the street ahead. Again, it was another street unfamiliar to me. But, the street after that was H. I turned to face the first street.

"Since it's late afternoon and the sun is in my face, I must be facing west."

"You're correct, Phil," my instructor, Jason, said.

"If you get in trouble," he continued, "ask a pedestrian. If no one responds, drop your harness and wait."

I grabbed the harness, slipped the strap between my fingers, took a breath and commanded Ladonna forward. We worked together and, at the end of our route, not only had we done perfectly, but I knew our pairing was a great one.

We met for the last time at our tables for dinner. Clare told us how proud she was of our accomplishments. She even said that we were all accomplished guide dog handlers. She told us some things to expect when we returned home, what obstacles we could encounter and how we needed to be aware of our surroundings.

"If you think you had problems here," she continued, "you'll encounter problems out there that you couldn't even imagine."

She stressed the importance of maintaining our dogs, specifically grooming, exercising and brushing teeth. She talked about graduation. "This will be your day," she said. "Tomorrow at 11:30, your puppy raisers will come to your room. You will let them play with your dog for about twenty minutes. From there you will go to the Dayroom and will have your pictures taken with your puppy raisers."

Once the photos were taken, we were to give our dogs to the puppy raisers until the ceremony, at which time we would be called to the graduation stage where our puppy raisers would present us with our dogs.

After dinner, one instructor guided me to a table with a giant card and placed Ladonna's left paw onto an ink pad and then onto the card. My signature went next to the paw print.

I hate goodbyes, yet I felt the need to stop by my classmates' rooms that evening. We talked for a few minutes and then said our goodbyes, promising to keep in touch.

The next morning, before the graduation briefing, we presented the instructors with our gifts: the card with all the signatures and paw prints and a large chocolate cake with red candy flowers, white candy dog bones and yellow dog biscuits.

Clare told me the family that raised Ladonna would be at my room at about 11:00 A.M. When they arrived, Ladonna went crazy; she reared back on her hind legs with her tail thumping the floor. It had been nearly a year since she had seen the Woods family, yet she seemed to recognize them.

The woman who raised Ladonna introduced herself to me and we shook hands. Then she introduced me to her sister, husband and daughter. The daughter, who was in middle school, gave me a brief history of Ladonna. She had taken Ladonna to picnics, sporting events and to her school's show and tell. Because of her temperament, the puppy raisers at the convention referred to Ladonna as "Miss Congeniality."

At 11:30, we went to the Dayroom and waited to be called for our photos. Mrs. Woods escorted Ladonna and I into the room where we would be photographed. The photographer took several pictures of the Woodses, Ladonna and myself. For my new photo ID, he sat me in a chair with Ladonna to my right, then, as he had done before, brought out his squeaky toy and whimpered and barked like a dog. After the photo, Ladonna's old owners escorted me to one of the tables in the graduation area. We sat and talked until 1:00, when I handed Ladonna's lead to Mrs. Woods and took my seat in the bleachers with the rest of the class.

Along with the students and puppy raisers, there were donors to Guide Dogs for the Blind from all over the country attending our graduation.

The CEO of Guide Dogs for the Blind welcomed everyone and gave a background talk about the organization. Our instructor gave a brief speech, then introduced Clare, who let out a nervous giggle and spoke about our class.

"When they arrived here October tenth," she said, "they were like deer in the headlights." She went on to talk about our training and about the rigorous schedule. Finally, she introduced class 649 to the audience. When it was my turn, Clare led me to the stage where the daughter of the family who had raised my dog presented me with Ladonna.

"Here, Philip." Someone handed me the microphone.

"I would just like to say that I came to San Rafael because it was the best school in the country." I paused. "I'd like to say that but that's not true. I thought, 'I'll go to California where it's warm to get away from the cold Wisconsin weather.'" I paused again. The comment drew sparse laughter. Then I praised the staff, from the dormitory services to the kitchen staff and the instructors. "Everything here is top line," I said. "This was an experience I will cherish for the rest of my life."

Everyone clapped. Clare, overcome with emotion, burst into tears.

"Ladonna," said the Woods' daughter, "was raised in Arizona and is now going to Wisconsin. I guess you could say that Ladonna is going from being a hot dog to a chilly dog." Even I had to chuckle at that one.

I reached out, grabbed Clare by the shoulders and gave her a big hug.

"Clare," I said, "you may not be the best guide dog instructor but I'd certainly rate you among the top eighty or ninety thousand."

"Oh," she said tearfully, "that's the nicest thing anyone has ever said to me."

It was nearly 4:00 P.M. when the event finally ended. We went to the cafeteria and sat talking and drinking coffee for about an hour. Then I returned to my room. Ladonna's original family gave me a photo album with pictures of Ladonna, a plastic bone and a rope toy, which they said was Ladonna's favorite. We hugged each other, said our goodbyes and promised to keep in touch.

Ladonna's principal trainer also stopped in to say goodbye and wish me luck. He wanted to see Ladonna one last time before we left. He bent over, stroked her chin and told me what a wonderful dog Ladonna was and how fortunate I was to have her.

"She had a great trainer," I said.

At 6:30, Ladonna and I entered the cafeteria for what would be our last official meal at Guide Dogs for the Blind.

The ride to the airport was uneventful and soon it was time for my plane to board. On the flight, I sat with Ladonna curled between my legs while I tried to nap. Several times, I dozed off and each time I awoke, I leaned down to feel my dog and she nuzzled against me.

I sat daydreaming about these four amazing weeks, what the future would be like with Ladonna and my family when, in one month, I would be retiring. What would be the next great adventure of my life?

Chapter 18

Ladonna Comes Home

T he pilot came on the loudspeaker: "Ladies and gentlemen, we will be arriving in Milwaukee in fifteen minutes."

"We'll be home soon, Ladonna," I said, stroking the neck of the beautiful yellow Labrador curled between my legs. I couldn't wait. It seemed like ages since I had been home. It had been quite an ordeal, twenty-eight straight days in the dormitory at the Guide Dogs for the Blind facility in San Rafael, California, twenty-eight days of intense training. But it was worth it: I had my guide dog, my main source of transportation and independence.

I leaned over and felt her satin-like ears. I couldn't wait to see my wife and kids and show off Ladonna.

"We are now landing in Milwaukee. The temperature is forty-five degrees," the flight attendant chirped.

The flight attendant waited until everyone was off the plane, then escorted Ladonna and me across the tarmac where a man met us at the terminal. He led me to a teary-eyed Donna who, along with my daughter, was waiting in the baggage claim area.

We exchanged hugs, walked to a grassy area to relieve Ladonna and headed home. I snuggled with Ladonna in the back seat while Donna drove the car and acted like a tour guide, describing the Milwaukee landmarks.

"Now we're at the Hoan bridge, the overpass, there's Lake Michigan and there's Miller Park."

Donna drove onto the Menomonee River Parkway, stopped and let Ladonna and I off at the bottom of the hill while she went to fetch Roxie, her four-month-old puppy. The guide instructors had advised me that when dogs meet for the first time, it should be at a neutral site; we chose the Menomonee River Parkway. With Ladonna at my side, I stood in the darkness listening to the wind brushing the trees and the sound of an occasional car cruising down the road. Suddenly, Ladonna reared up and lunged forward, wagging her tail furiously. It was Donna and Roxie crossing the road. Donna and I stood about three feet apart while the two dogs pawed and circled each other.

With Donna and Roxie in the lead, we crossed the road and walked up the hill to our house. Donna took Roxie to the back yard while I commanded Ladonna up the four steps and onto the front porch.

"This is your new home, Ladonna," I told her.

The next morning, I eagerly returned to work at the Department of Aging, this time to show off my new companion. It was unbelievable. People whom I didn't know sought me out, because they wanted to meet Ladonna, to stroke her beautiful blond fur and those honey-colored, satin-like ears.

"I should have gotten one of these dogs years ago," I told one coworker.

I spent the entire day parading my new prize from room to room, from cubicle to cubicle, introducing Ladonna to coworkers and supervisors.

During the afternoon, our union president and the union treasurer stopped into my office. The president sat on the floor stroking Ladonna's face and her chin and rubbing her belly. Even my former officemate complimented me on my new companion.

My first task with Ladonna was to train her to find our house. That would be accomplished by "back chaining," that is, standing by the steps directly in front of the house. First, I gave her a kibble, stroked her, then stepped backward a few paces. From there, I commanded her forward to the steps and gave her another kibble. Each time, I stepped further backward until I reached the end of the block. When she returned to the steps, I rewarded Ladonna with more kibble. I continued with the exercise until I felt certain that she could find the house.

On January 3 we took our first Milwaukee route together. From our house, we went down 83rd, turned right and continued up Warren, made a right onto Church, went down Milwaukee Avenue and then back down 83rd to the house; Ladonna behaved perfectly.

California-bred and Arizona-raised, I wondered how Ladonna would react to Wisconsin's harsh winters, particularly snow. When playing, she romped, jumped, slid and rolled as if she had been around snow all her life. When in harness, it was a different story. After the first snowfall that January, she led me to an area with which I was unfamiliar.

After about twenty minutes of jumping up and down and screaming while in the middle of the street, I managed to flag down a passing motorist.

"Sir, sir," I shouted, "can you tell me where the hell I am?"

"Jackson Park Boulevard."

Jackson Park—it was six blocks from where I thought I was.

Twice, during routes that winter, I fell. The first time occurred on Warren Street when I tripped over a bump hidden beneath a blanket of snow; the other incident occurred on Woodland when I hit the hard pavement after slipping on a patch of black ice. Each time, I managed to hang onto the leash. The staff at Guide Dogs for the Blind constantly warned us about hanging on to the leash: "You can let go of the harness, but never, I mean never, let go of the leash!"

Unlike normal dogs, guide dogs who spend a lot of time working in harness want to let loose—they will take off any chance they get. Four times, Ladonna managed to escape from our fenced-in backyard. Three times, within an hour or two at the most, she was brought back by someone in the neighborhood. The fourth time, however, was different. Ten minutes after letting the two dogs out into the backyard, I went to check on them. Both were gone.

I called and called to the dogs—no response. To my horror, I found the backyard gate, which I always locked, had been opened. Apparently, after spraying the back lawn, the man from our lawn service had left the gate open. Frantically, I ran to the front yard and called out for Ladonna. A few minutes later, I heard what sounded like a dog running toward me—it was a dog, all right, but not the one I wanted; it was Roxie. I called and called out to Ladonna; no response. Some buddies of mine, several neighbors and even the police scoured the area but could not locate Ladonna.

"I saw a large yellow dog cross Milwaukee Avenue," a construction worker said.

Crossing Milwaukee Avenue? I worried she could get hit by a car, or worse, a bus!

With Roxie sprawled next to me, I sat and waited for a sign, hoping for a rap at the door or the phone to ring. On one hand, I wanted the phone to ring, yet on the other hand I didn't. A phone call could mean one of two things: Ladonna was found and safe or Ladonna was seriously injured or worse. After five hours I had given up hope of ever being reunited with my beautiful yellow Lab. Then Roxie sprang up from her spot on the floor, bolted to the door and started barking. What could she be barking at? As far as I could tell, there was no one on the front porch or even on the front walk. Could it be? I took a deep breath and slowly opened the front door; there was Ladonna, brushing against my left thigh. I knew I should have scolded her, but I just couldn't. Instead, I dropped to my knees, broke into tears and embraced her. From that day forward, I always checked the back gate three or four times before letting her out.

One month after my graduation from Guide Dogs for the Blind, Ladonna was at my side when I attended the wedding of the right fielder on my 2004 championship softball team. Many of the guests marveled at how composed the beautiful yellow Lab was as she sat while they stomped to the loud music. That was the first of five weddings to which Ladonna accompanied me.

That September, I audited five classes at the University of Wisconsin-Milwaukee. Along with my friend, Ladonna was a student in my philosophy class and the other four we audited.

In May 2006, she accompanied me on the train to Chicago to attend my son's graduation from The University of Illinois-Chicago. She was flawless on the hectic platform at Chicago's Union Station, weaving me through the stampede of passersby.

She sat as proudly as I did as my son received his Master's degree. In August, we took her on her first of about one hundred trips to our cabin in Three Lakes, Wisconsin. A treacherous, winding, narrow rocky stairway led down from the house, but Ladonna always managed to lead me safely down the steep bluff and onto the beach below. While Donna and the children played fetch with Roxie in the water, Ladonna remained on shore, tethered to the picnic table with a long cable—I was not going to risk her running off into the woods.

"If she takes off, you may never see her again," guide instructor Lauren Ross had warned me.

Ladonna wasn't denied lake privileges, of course. Her tether was long enough to get her in up to her belly. And after swimming laps, I often took her into the shallow water on leash.

Ladonna and I went everywhere together, whether it was a trek around the neighborhood, to my Thursday breakfast at the sandwich shop with my buddies, to the restaurant after our softball games and even to the dentist, which was located a good two miles from home. At medical appointments, she'd lay on the floor untethered and off leash and harness, staring at me. She'd often raise her right eyebrow while my internist gave me the once over. It was as if she was saying, "What are you doing to my master?"

Ladonna and I were constantly together. We were a team. Ladonna was popular and well known around my favorite haunts.

"Hello, Ladonna," was the familiar greeting when we entered a restaurant or pub. As far as they were concerned, I was that guy, "what's his name," tagging along. She was the star of our show.

She was at every softball practice and every ballgame. It was Ladonna who led me to the pitcher's mound for the pregame meetings with the umpire and opposing manager. No matter what the weather, she sat calmly next to me while I kicked the dirt and barked out instructions to the players on the field. After the games, we were back on the mound; this time, getting high-fived by the team we had just beaten. After the games,

Ladonna led me up the ramp and to our table at our favorite post-game restaurant. While my players and I were laughing and telling tales of the game, Ladonna was under the table sipping ice water.

She wasn't merely a guide dog or a companion, but a family member; I often referred to her as my fourth child. She came to my daughter's piano recitals and her graduation from The Maryland Institute of Art. She attended my other daughter's ballet and modern dance recitals in both Milwaukee and Minneapolis. She was at my side when I gave a short speech at my son's wedding and there she was, sitting with me in the audience at the school plays Donna directed.

During those early times with Ladonna at my side, I shared my story at colleges, senior centers and grade schools, telling people about how I not only coped with my blindness, but thrived. Afterward, Ladonna and I would show the audience how guide dogs and their masters operated. I loved being able to educate people about being blind and how, with hard work, a person could still be a valuable, contributing member of society. Ladonna helped show that a blind person could have a partner—a friend—there every step of the way!

We were featured together on two television programs, "A Coach's Blind Ambition" and "Blind Coach Sees Challenges."

In or out of harness, Ladonna was always fiesty. Her routes were flawless; she guided me from point A to point B, led me up and down stairs, halted me at curbs, guided me across busy intersections, warned me about overhanging objects like tree branches, steered me around toys like coaster wagons and tricycles, around trash-cans and cars blocking the sidewalks; she always led me back home safely.

She was even with us when we all met in Atlanta, Georgia, to spend Thanksgiving with my son, his wife and my granddaughter, who loves stroking Ladonna's chin and tugging on that beautiful long, bushy tail, just like I do. If it was an important moment in my life, Ladonna was by my side. She would accompany me when we embarked on our next adventure together: my retirement.

Chapter 19

Retirement

W ith Ladonna at my side, I strolled through the lobby of my office building for the last time.

One of the secretaries whom I had known for years greeted me and walked with me to my office. "Is this your last day?" she asked. I nodded but couldn't speak. I had mixed feelings. Although I was ready to retire, I felt a sadness. After thirty-three years, I was leaving for good.

Though I couldn't see, I switched on the lights and felt along the ledge of the bulletin board. Everything was gone; the family and team photos, team trophies and cartoons. All that remained were two file cabinets and my desk with the computer equipment.

It was time to clean out my office. I grabbed papers from the bottom drawer and stuffed them into the wastebasket. There were folders with memos I saved but had never read, grievances I had filed, reprimands I had been issued, evaluations and old time sheets. There were thirty-three years of memories in those drawers and it was hard to discard them.

Ladonna, relaxing under my desk, became curious. She crept toward the wastebasket to see what was going on. She was undoubtedly looking for something to eat.

The union president and treasurer stopped in to see me—I thought mainly to see my guide dog.

"You're not really retiring?" she asked in a raspy voice.

"Yep, I really am."

She told me she was sad I was leaving and I told her it was time. She asked me what I was going to do after retiring.

"I'm going to do nothing—just vegetate."

She knelt down and stroked Ladonna's belly. We talked about the state of Milwaukee County and about the union. She wasn't sure if she would seek another term as union president. We reminisced some more, but then it was time for her to go.

I walked her to the door, gave her a big hug and told her I would call her.

Ladonna and I strolled down the corridor past the cubicles and offices, many of which were empty. It was an eerie feeling, not hearing the conversations of workers, not hearing the phones constantly ringing or the sounds of papers being shuffled—it was like being in a cemetery. How different it was from my first day at the welfare building back in 1973: workers sitting at desks in a large room—the supervisors were in cubicles in the rear. It was always bustling, with the shuffling of feet on the tile floor, the constant ringing of phones and the chattering of coworkers. The large room was bright and the desks were close together. There was no air conditioning. On those hot summer days, windows were open and on windy days, papers blew across the desks while the aromas of chocolate and hops from the brewery next door saturated the room.

We were young, idealistic and ready to save the world. There was a camaraderie of workers, lost with the move to the Schlitz Building with its cubicles, offices and stifling air.

It was after 3:30 when Donna and my daughter arrived. Donna went through my file cabinet and my daughter through my desk drawers. Then we went through my computer files to make sure there wasn't anything of a personal nature on my computer. At about 4:15, I turned off the light for the last time.

On New Year's Eve day, my first full day of retirement, Ladonna and I went for a walk around the block. Ladonna was perfect and I decided to extend the walk to three blocks, which meant going north to Woodland Street. On the three-block walk I got lost; I had miscounted the number of streets between Church Street and 83rd Street. We made a wrong turn and went north instead of south on 83rd Street. Sensing something was wrong, I flagged down a passing motorist, just like Clare and my instructor Jason had told me to do during my training. The man in the car identified the street and I then corrected Ladonna and, together, we went back home. It was like self-orientation all over again.

To a dog who was born in California and raised in Arizona, snow naturally became a problem. Snowbanks covered the down curbs, forcing Ladonna to go over or around them. Once we went around an ice bank and ended up in the street. I turned her, walked along the edge of the snow bank and found my way back to the curb.

Adapting to icy sidewalks became a challenge. We'd start out slipping and sliding but usually managed to stay on our feet. However, on one particularly cold morning, I tripped over a bump hidden beneath the two inches of snow on the sidewalk. I hit the ground hard on my right side but managed to hold on to the harness and leash. Although the bump has since been removed, Ladonna still comes to a complete stop at that exact spot, her way of telling me that she still remembers the fall.

When at Guide Dogs for the Blind, we were exposed to every kind of obstacle we might encounter with our dogs. Yet Clare warned us that when we returned home with our dogs, we would encounter all kinds of obstacles and that we had better be prepared for them.

That was the case in April when Ladonna and I took a jaunt north down 83rd Street. After we crossed Woodland, she veered left and onto the curbside grass. I halted her, then commanded her left, but she wouldn't move. I felt there was something wrong but I didn't know what it was. *I'll leave it up to her*, I thought, so I commanded her forward. She veered to the left and around an object, then made a sharp turn to the right and led me up someone's lawn.

"Hey you," shouted a man from behind me. "Don't move!"

He charged over to me and told me that they were cutting down trees and that my dog had led me around some logs and machinery.

"We have a sign up, a warning sign that no one was to enter this area but your dog took you right past that sign."

"Well," I said, "This dog can take me across streets, around and under objects, up and down stairs and into elevators. But there's one thing she still hasn't learned yet."

"What's that?" the man asked.

"She still hasn't learned how to read."

To my amazement and to the astonishment of Lauren Ross, a Field Manager for Guide Dogs for the Blind, Ladonna did something extraordinary for a guide dog, something she was not trained to do. On Thursdays, Ladonna and I would meet my friend Tim in front of my house and together we walked to a sandwich shop to join other friends for our traditional breakfast. Since Tim, who fears most large dogs and was especially leery of Roxie, my pet dog, did not want to enter the house, we set up a system where he would ring me twice on his cell phone, at which time I would join him outside. On a Thursday morning in November of 2010, forty-five minutes before I was to meet Tim, I had gone into the basement to retrieve a sweatshirt from the dryer. Halfway down the steps, Roxie leaped onto the open door and slammed it shut, which resulted in my being locked in the basement. At first, I contemplated emulating John Wayne by kicking down the door. *Wait a minute*, I thought, *why not just wait for Tim?* When I don't answer the door after his two rings, he'll surely enter the house and free me from the basement. Sure enough, it was about forty minutes later when I heard the two rings. As usual, Roxie bolted to the front door, barking furiously. A few minutes later, I heard the barking along with footsteps in the kitchen. Thank God, it was Tim, who opened the basement door and let me out. To my amazement, it wasn't Roxie but Ladonna standing at the basement door barking. Tim told me he knew I was in trouble when he peeked through the window and saw Ladonna barking. She not only continued barking after he entered the house, but led him into the kitchen and to the basement door.

"It was like Lassie finding Timmy," said Tim.

"She's not trained to do that," Lauren, who recounted the incident to the instructors at Guide Dogs for the Blind in San Rafael, told me.

In May 2014, I gave a dog presentation for Donna's first grade class. I demonstrated the obedience and guide commands and walked Ladonna around obstacles, through doorways and up and down stairs.

"How does it feel to be blind?" asked one little boy.

Slowly I replied, "It's something I have learned to get used to."

Epilogue

Even post-retirement, I continued to have adventures. I genuinely love softball and continued to coach after retirement. During our 2013 season, one of my players, Christina, told me that she had once been an employee of Fox Television.

"I told them about my coach being blind," she said. "They were excited and want to do a feature about you."

I asked myself why Fox would want to do a story about a blind softball coach. The following Wednesday, the day before our next game, a reporter and news anchor from Fox telephoned me.

"We'd like to cover your game tomorrow night," he said. "Christina told me all about you and your team and we feel it would be a strong human interest segment."

After our conversation, I immediately called everyone on the team to tell them that they would be on TV.

"Be sure to get there early and be sure to wear your team shirts," I said.

The day of the game dawned cold, misty and windy. The field was in terrible condition for a game, but I knew my team would step up.

Moments after arriving, I was greeted by the reporter I'd spoken with on the phone and a cameraman. We talked about my life and how, despite being blind, I could still coach my team and inspire them to win. Then he went around talking to some of the players while I went over the lineup. I heard one player tell the reporter about how I recruited the players, held the practices and, from memory, made out the lineups.

The cameraman slipped a microphone around my neck; we were ready to go. I stood there, poised, with Ladonna by my side.

In order to capture my shenanigans during the game as well as the ball crossing home plate, Fox employed two cameras: one mounted at the backstop on the third base side and one pointing directly toward me.

"Let's put up some runs," I shouted, clapping my hands. "Let's get five."

We started with a double off the fence. My new leftfielder followed with a second double and another player blasted a long home run over the centerfield wall. By the time the first inning ended, we were up 13–0.

When we were in the field, I'd turn to my right, cup my hands and shout out instructions to the players: "Guard the line. Shift to the right. Force play at third," and so on.

We had never played better. Due to the forty-five minute time limit, the ump halted the game in the sixth inning; the score was 26–3 in our favor.

After the game, the reporter set out to interview the players. What he wanted was accounts from the veteran players who had been on the team for years. He started with Jack, who was in his seventeenth year with the team. After his interview, Jack told me that he had said some great things about me.

"Just like you wrote it up," he said, laughing.

From Jack the reporter went to Becky, who was so excited she could barely speak. "He's very competitive, very, very competitive," she said.

During the interviews, I stood listening, pride blooming in my chest. After Becky, he interviewed Tyler, who I consider the greatest player I have ever coached. With the camera rolling, the usually unflappable Tyler choked. Tyler, who had been on the team for six years, told the reporter he had been a member of the team for fifteen years.

Then the reporter approached me. It was my turn. Somehow I made it through the interview. He compared my attitude and history of winning to that of the legendary Green Bay Packers coach Vince Lombardi. He was particularly impressed with my record which, at that time, was two hundred thirty-seven wins and thirty-six losses with twelve championship titles. He even went so far as to say I had a dynasty. But he was most fascinated by how I accomplished our team's record and coached the players so skillfully without sight. I said I achieved it all through careful listening.

"If someone curses and tosses their bat, I know they struck out," I joked.

The segment, "Blind Softball Coach Sees Success Despite Challenges," aired June 23, 2013. Many of the players were ecstatic seeing themselves on TV. Ladonna even managed to get her beautiful face into the segment.

"The gruff sixty-eight-year-old skipper," the reporter narrated, "prowls the dugout with his pooch, a guide dog named Ladonna."

It was the perfect complement to a rewarding experience, because it included Ladonna. Through thick and thin, through softball games and everyday life, my companion—my friend—Ladonna was always by my side.

Acknowledgments

When I first embarked on becoming a published author, I was told that the odds were at least one-thousand-to-one against me. That assessment was correct, in that I sent out over one thousand query letters to both publishers and agents and received over one thousand rejections. That, however, did not discourage me. After all, throughout my seventy plus years of life, I often defied the odds—the more I was told I couldn't do something, the more determined I was to prove those naysayers wrong.

The writing in itself was not the most difficult part in the process; in fact, I had more fun writing about my life than actually living it.

Notwithstanding all the effort I put into this project, I couldn't have reached my goal without the assistance of others.

First, of course, is my beautiful bride of forty-one years, Donna, whose support, inspiration and assistance with the manuscript, the query letters and the proposal guided me through this arduous process. Then there are my children, Nicholas, Michelle and Rebecca, who like Donna advised and guided me and helped format the manuscript. In addition, I'm grateful to Carolyn Kott Washburne, an adjunct associate professor in the Department of English at the University of Wisconsin-Milwaukee, who instructed me during my early attempts to get published.

Despite my efforts and the assistance of others, my dream would never have become a reality without Dr. Joan Dunphy, the publisher and editor-in-chief of New Horizon Press, who committed her resources to enable an unknown blind guy like me to become a published author. I'm also grateful to JoAnne Thomas, vice president of finance and marketing at New Horizon Press, for not only promoting *Binoculars*, but putting up with my many obnoxious phone calls. Also, I thank Caroline Russomanno and Charley Nasta who, along with Joan, brilliantly edited *Binoculars*, which was no easy task.

I'm also indebted to Lauren Ross, field manager for Guide Dogs for the Blind. During our ten-year association, her instruction enabled me to become a proficient and confident guide dog handler. After the death of my first guide dog, she provided the support I needed to get through that crisis. Despite her many obligations, she took time to write the foreword for this book.

Last, I'm eternally grateful to my mentor and agent, Maryann Karinch. Had it not been for her, I'd still be stranded in oblivion like countless other individuals hoping, waiting and praying to become published authors. Despite her many commitments, she always advised me, counseled me and took the time to reply to my ridiculous e-mails. Not only did she guide me through the writing of the manuscript and the proposal, but continuously encouraged and inspired me. "You can do this; I know you can," she told me when I was faltering. After that encouragement, I knew I was well on my way and nothing was going to stop me.